SURVIVING ZOMBIE WARFARE

ZOMBIE SPOTTING AND SURVIVAL BASICS

SEAN T. PAGE

ROSEN
PUBLISHING®
New York

IMPORTANT

YOU MUST READ THE FOLLOWING BEFORE CONTINUING

In a recent international survey, more than 63% of people believed that within the next decade the world would be facing a zombie apocalypse – when the shuffling dead emerge in such numbers that our civilisation is simply overwhelmed.

However, all is not lost. You hold in your hands one of the most comprehensive survival manuals ever produced. Richly illustrated and packed with the latest scientific updates, it will take you through everything you need to know to stay alive when the rest of the world is being feasted upon. From what a zombie is and where they come from, to how to kill them and develop your own survival plan, it's all in this volume, which I hope will become a well-used guide as you prepare to face the walking dead. This book is designed to educate, train, amuse, scare and prepare, and not always in that order.

If you currently consider yourself an 'unbeliever', welcome also and read on. For within these pages you'll find detailed and documented evidence of zombie outbreaks through history as well as corroborated scientific proof that the zombie virus and zombies exist. We are fortunate to have had exclusive access to the scientist many consider to be the founding father of zombiology, Dr Khalid Ahmed.

But, don't worry, this isn't just a text book. There's a stack of information on innovative ways to take out zombies and some downright dangerous advice on everything from creating a zombie-busting wheelchair to building devastating traps to ensnare the walking dead.

And, at the back, there is a chance to test your knowledge and become a certified zombie survivalist. Now that will be something to tell them about at school or add to your CV.

If you've been scared by zombie films, been kept up at night by zombie books, or just have an unhealthy fear that the world is about to end, and that zombies will most certainly have a role in it, then this is the book for you.

Finally, don't be ashamed that you are only now learning about zombies. Read this book in public, let folks see you are concerned about the dead. You'll be surprised how many will tap you on the shoulder and say 'hey, I'm worried about zombies too'. It can be a real eye-opener and a great way to make some unusual new friends.

By picking up this Haynes manual you've taken the first step to saying 'I will survive the zombies', so read on, make notes in the margins, scribble things on bits of paper and start making your own plans. Things are about to get very strange.

Sean T. Page
Ministry of Zombies, London

This edition published in 2017 by:

The Rosen Publishing Group, Inc.
29 East 21st Street
New York, NY 10010

Library of Congress Cataloging-in-Publication Data

Names: Page, Sean T.
Title: Zombie spotting and survival basics / Sean T. Page.
Description: New York : Rosen Pub., 2017. | Series: Surviving zombie warfare | Includes bibliographical references and index.
Identifiers: LCCN 2016002168|
ISBN 9781499463835 (library bound)
ISBN 9781499463811 (pbk.)
ISBN 9781499463828 (6-pack)
Subjects: LCSH: Zombies--Humor.
Classification: LCC PN6231.Z65 P34 2016 | DDC 818/.602--dc23
LC record available at http://lccn.loc.gov/2016002168

Manufactured in the United States of America

Originally published in English by Haynes Publishing under the title: Zombie Survival Manual © Sean T. Page 2013.

CONTENTS

WHAT IS A ZOMBIE? — 6

TYPES OF ZOMBIE — 8
HOW TO KILL A ZOMBIE — 10

THE SCIENCE OF ZOMBIOLOGY — 12

RESEARCH IN A CRISIS — 14
BUILDING A SECRET LAB — 16
THE ZOMBIE VIRUS AND ANIMALS — 18

ZOMBIES IN HISTORY — 20

HISTORICAL ACCOUNTS — 22
THE ZOMBIE APOCALYPSE — 24

BECOMING A ZOMBIE SURVIVALIST — 26

GETTING THE LOOK — 28
BE READY OR BE DEAD! — 30
ANTI-ZOMBIE PRODUCTS — 34
BUILD YOUR OWN SURVIVOR TEAM — 36

ZOMBIE SURVIVAL EXAMS — 38

GLOSSARY — 42

FOR MORE INFORMATION — 43

FOR FURTHER READING — 45

INDEX — 46

WHAT IS A ZOMBIE?

Before beginning any reading or course in zombie survival, it is essential that you have a clear understanding of what a zombie is, how it is created, the main types and, most important of all, how you can 'kill' a zombie.

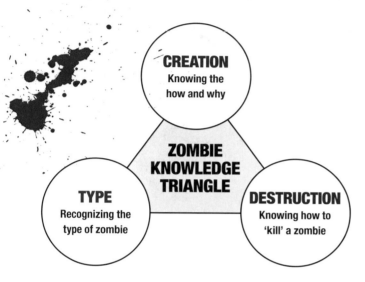

ZOMBIE KNOWLEDGE TRIANGLE

CREATION
Knowing the how and why

TYPE
Recognizing the type of zombie

DESTRUCTION
Knowing how to 'kill' a zombie

These three factors are the foundation of any zombie survival plan and are referred to as the Zombie Knowledge Triangle. All zombie survivalists must clearly understand how a zombie is created, be able to recognize the different types and deal with the walking dead.

> **A ZOMBIE IS A DEAD BODY THAT HAS BEEN BROUGHT BACK TO ANIMATION BY A COMPLEX RNA VIRUS WHICH LEADS THE BODY TO BEHAVE IN A CANNIBALISTIC WAY**
>
> MINISTRY OF ZOMBIES HANDBOOK

To be clear, the zombic condition, which is characterized by the slow stagger, lumbering walk and violent appetite for the flesh of the living, are all classic symptoms of the zombie virus. So, there is nothing supernatural, nothing spooky and nothing superhuman about the walking dead. They are simply humans transformed into very different creatures. But always remember that once a human has become infected with the virus, typically by a bite from an infected zombie, then the transformation will begin. More detail is given on this process further in this volume but know this:

THERE IS CURRENTLY NO CURE FOR THE ZOMBIE VIRUS AND ONCE CONTRACTED BY A HUMAN, TRANSFORMATION INTO A ZOMBIE IS A CERTAINTY

WHAT IS A ZOMBIE?
ZOMBIE CREATION MYTHS

In a recent survey by GeoPol, fewer than 23% of Americans realized that zombism is caused by a virus. Here is a breakdown that shows the level of misunderstanding among the public of the root cause of zombies.

29.3% VOODOO
Magic, myth and the poison from the rare puffer fish leads to mindless undead slaves.

22.8% VIRUS
The world of science has the answer – it's caused by a virus.

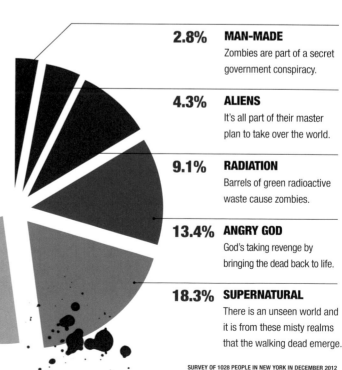

2.8% MAN-MADE
Zombies are part of a secret government conspiracy.

4.3% ALIENS
It's all part of their master plan to take over the world.

9.1% RADIATION
Barrels of green radioactive waste cause zombies.

13.4% ANGRY GOD
God's taking revenge by bringing the dead back to life.

18.3% SUPERNATURAL
There is an unseen world and it is from these misty realms that the walking dead emerge.

SURVEY OF 1028 PEOPLE IN NEW YORK IN DECEMBER 2012

► HOW TO SPOT A ZOMBIE

KNOW THE SIGNS!

Scruffy Bohemian student or 'back from the office late' drone may each display signs of the zombic condition, but it doesn't necessarily mean you should run and get the axe. It is vital that you clearly identify your target as a zombie before you get chopping. Be on the lookout for the following:

► A vacant and distant gaze, which only becomes agitated at the prospect of living flesh. The creature will emit a low-level guttural groan.

► A pallid, deathly colorless skin. Eyes may be milky or tinged with red. Both nails and hair may have grown giving the figure a distinctive 'hippie' look and smell.

► Clothes may be ripped or torn. There may be obvious injuries such as clear bite marks or missing limbs, but equally there may be no visible signs of trauma or dried blood.

► Slow, stumbling walk. Zombies appear unbalanced and awkward, often tripping and falling over minor obstacles. Newly converted zombies will display a better level of movement and dexterity.

► The walking dead will always move towards the living with the express purpose of turning them into their next meat snack.

BE WARNED CITIZENS!

WHAT IS A ZOMBIE?

TYPES OF ZOMBIE

Once a human has turned into a zombie, they will enter a three-stage process of transformation. All will go through these stages, but factors such as climate, body mass and the amount of infected material will have an impact.

To be clear, these are not stages of the 'illness' – these will be reviewed later. For now, these humans have already transformed into the undead, they are fully infected with zombie virus and display symptoms of the zombic condition. In 2008, Dr Ahmed shocked the zombie-fighting community when he declared that 'all zombies are not equal.' He later went on to expand on a scientific theory of zombie evolution, which describes how the undead develop over the course of time after infection. For many years, survivalists had offered accounts of desiccated zombies or huge bloated corpse-monsters, but the fledging science of Zombiology had no unified theory to explain these anomalies. Dr Ahmed's stages of zombie evolution changed all of this and they are presented below.

▶ ZOMBIE EVOLUTION

◀ STAGE 1
FRESH
(NOOBS, NEWBIES, INHUMOS)

These walking dead have contracted the zombie virus in the last few days. They have a pallid, gray/blue skin color and a bloodless complexion. Some will appear almost human in appearance; others will be missing major body parts. Importantly, their movements will be stiff and awkward, they will be unable to speak and they will have an unhealthy interest in feasting on your flesh.

▶ STAGE 2
PUTREFIED
(SICKIES, PUKERS, FATTIES, BUG BOYS, BLOATERS)

At this stage, zombies generally start to show signs of decomposition. For example, you may see pus-filled wounds and green fungus patches appearing. However, the decomposition process is greatly decelerated by the zombic condition. In humid conditions, excess acid or gastric liquid may swell the corpse to an enormous size.

WHAT IS A ZOMBIE?
CLIMATIC CONDITIONS

Experiments have now proved that it is climatic conditions which have the greatest influence on the 'type' of creature that survivors will face after Z-Day. For example, fighters in hot and humid, tropical or sub-tropical climates are likely to face more putrefied and bloated zombies whereas fighters in arid and desert conditions will battle dried and skeletal ghouls.

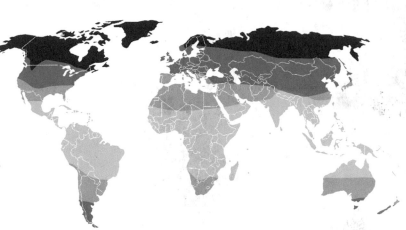

■ TUNDRA		■ DESERT	
■ TEMPERATE		■ TROPICAL	

▶ **STAGE 3**
DESICCATED
(CLASSICS, ZEDS, STIFFS, STENCHIES, HIPPIES)

Most of the walking dead will move into this 'classic' zombie phase of development. These creatures will be barely human in appearance. Their skin will be thin and stretched; their wounds dry and cracked. By this stage, their clothes will be mostly tattered and their eyes turned a milky shade, even yellowish in some cases. Climatic conditions will determine the actual level of moisture in a classic zombie, with dry conditions leading to a skeletal creature on which the skin hangs like a rotting, almost transparent blanket. Over time, injury or rotten body parts may just fall off with the creature seemingly oblivious to any loss.

ONCE INFECTED BY BITE OR FLUID EXCHANGE, A HUMAN WILL TRANSFORM INTO A ZOMBIE AND MOVE THROUGH THESE ZOMBIE TYPES

TROPICAL High temperature, high humidity

Bloated masses of dead flesh in addition to a veritable explosion in the insect life and fungus surrounding these walking corpses.

▶ High numbers of 'bloaters'.
▶ Higher rate of decomposition.
▶ More fungal growth.

DESERT High temperature, low humidity

Often referred to as 'skeleton corpses', the dead will be thin and wiry with more exposed bone than in other regions.

▶ Parched zombies.
▶ Skeletal husks.
▶ Bleached flesh stretched tightly.

TEMPERATE Low temperature, high humidity

Survivors should prepare to face all types of zombie in the initial outbreak. Depending on the season, most will move towards the classic phase.

▶ Most zombies will be at the desiccated stage within a month.
▶ Fewer bloaters than the tropics.

TUNDRA Low temperature, low humidity

Winter will often keep the dead fully frozen and easy to deal with, but the thaw can see zombies emerge in a particularly rotten and hungry mood.

▶ Zombies may be frozen solid and dormant.
▶ Very low level of decomposition.

WHAT IS A ZOMBIE?

HOW TO KILL A ZOMBIE

Weapons and more advanced unarmed combat techniques that can be used against the dead will be discussed later. For now it's enough to know that to kill a zombie you must destroy at least 80% of its brain. Nothing else will work. In zombie combat, we define 'killing' a zombie as meaning removing it as a threat – in other words, taking it out of the game by ensuring that it never gets up. Technically speaking, you can't 'kill' what's already dead, but destroying a high proportion of a zombie's brain will prevent the creature rising again and seeking to feast on the flesh of the living.

A BLOW WHICH DOES NOT CONNECT SQUARELY WITH THE ZOMBIE SKULL WILL NOT DO ENOUGH DAMAGE SO PRACTICE YOUR ACCURACY

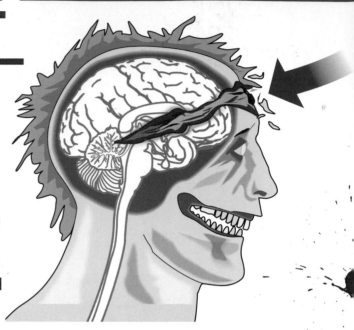

▶ A TYPICAL THREE-STEP PROCEDURE

STEP 1
IDENTIFY THE ZOMBIE

Recognize the creature, shout a warning if you can, then get prepared for action! Remember, the zombie in front of you is no longer human so act with purpose. Do not endanger yourself with any warning; there may be occasions when you need to move quickly through Step 1.

STEP 2
HEAD BASH OR KNOCK DOWN

If you have a weapon, go for a solid club to the head. Aim for the top of the skull and use force but be accurate – a glancing blow may not do the trick. If you are unarmed, you will need to sweep the creature's legs or kick it down. Remember, only a solid blow to the head will knock the creature down for good.

⚠ WHAT IS A ZOMBIE?
COMMON MISCONCEPTIONS

More than any creature, the zombie is surrounded by legend, myth and misinformation. The zombie survivalist needs to be aware of these misconceptions. During the zombie apocalypse, panic and lies will be everywhere, rumors of their superpowers will be rife, and such tales will haunt the dreams of any survivors.

AREN'T THEY JUST LIKE VAMPIRES?

Vampires are fictional monsters based on a mixture of folklore and creative writing. They have no connection to zombies. There is nothing sparkly or romantic about 'the undead' and you won't be joining 'Team Edward' or 'Team Jacob' when the dead rise. You're more likely to be driving an axe through his skull than losing yourself in his good looks.

SHOULD I STAY AWAY FROM CEMETERIES?

For the seasoned zombie fighter, a cemetery should hold none of the horror it seems to for fans of ghost or vampire stories. It is a virus which causes the zombic condition. There is nothing supernatural about it and, statistically, very few zombies 'rise from the grave'. The incubation period for the virus means that there are far more outbreaks in hospital morgues than in chapels of rest or graveyards.

DON'T ZOMBIES JUST EAT BRAINS?

The most powerful myth surrounding zombies is that they only eat brains. Indeed, the classic "Brraaaaiinnss!" catchphrase supposedly muttered by the dead could seriously mislead survivors. Firstly, zombies will happily eat any part of a living or very recently deceased human. Secondly, zombies cannot talk.

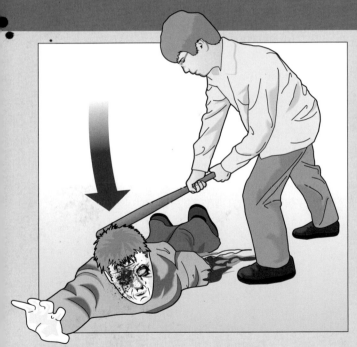

STEP 3
SECOND BLOW OR STAMP

Zombies are extremely robust creatures, so always be sure by delivering a second blow. Never assume that your one hit has done the job. Many an experienced zombie fighter has been bitten on the lower leg by a ghoul they thought they'd dealt with. For once, the movies got it right – always use the double-tap rule.

IF THEY ARE FRIENDS OR FAMILY, SURELY THEY'LL KNOW WHO I AM?

Simple answer, no! Once a human has transformed into a zombie, they have virtually no recollection of their former life. They are no longer the person they once were. So if zombie grandma staggers into view, it won't be to drop off any last-minute birthday or Christmas presents. Do not be deceived by the physical resemblance to your loved one. It's time to get busy with the axe. The zombic condition completely transforms any human into a ravenous and cannibalistic creature, and scientific experiments have shown that zombies will attack and feast upon the living, no matter who they are. It may not be easy driving a weapon into your neighbor's face or bashing a friend in with a baseball bat, so if necessary get someone else to do it. But, be assured, if you don't deal with zombie grandma, she will come drooling at the window. Finally, never attempt to bring a relative with the zombic condition into your fortified home. Where a member of your party has become infected, you should isolate them and then deal with them when they turn if you can't do it beforehand.

ANY BLOW TO A ZOMBIE HEAD WILL RESULT IN INFECTED BRAIN SPLATTER. BE ALERT TO THE RISK OF INFECTION

THE SCIENCE OF ZOMBIOLOGY

The fledgling science of zombiology is the study of both the zombie virus itself and the associated zombic condition it causes in humans. Although still largely discounted by mainstream academics, more and more research is being conducted into this area.

After an intensive period of field work in northwest India between 1997 and 2001, it was microbiologist and anthropologist Dr Khalid Ahmed who first isolated the complex RNA virus that triggers the development of the zombic condition. He became the first to fully document the virus and the remarkably metamorphosing effect it has on the human brain and body.

Since 2002, Dr Ahmed's research has been supported and developed by institutions and individuals around the world, but there are still many unanswered questions in the science of zombiology. For example, the biology behind certain zombie types such as the 'snapper', which is an infected head that has been separated from the body and yet continues to live and try to consume human flesh. However, the single greatest obstacle to scientific progress in the field of zombiology is the opposition and downright hostility of the world's universities and the research community in general.

THERE IS CURRENTLY NO CURE FOR THE ZOMBIE VIRUS. DO NOT BE MISLED BY CLAIMS OF A CURE. INFECTION WILL LEAD TO THE ZOMBIC CONDITION

▶ 4 STAGES OF TRANSFORMATION

Many factors affect the rate at which a human will move through the transformation stages to develop the full-blown zombic condition. The critical factors are the quantity of infected material transferred and the size and health of the infected individual.

There have been cases where a fully grown adult with only a small infected scratch lasted over 24 hours before becoming a zombie.

In other studies, major wounds such as a zombie bite to the jugular has seen humans transforming within minutes rather than hours.

1 INFECTION
1–4 HOURS

▶ Raised temperature and flu-like symptoms.
▶ Excessive sweating.
▶ Panic attacks.
▶ An infected individual may hide any symptoms or be unaware that they have been infected.
▶ As the zombic condition develops, there will be a noticeable lack of appetite.

2 FLU SYMPTOMS
2–8 HOURS

▶ Continuation of flu-like symptoms.
▶ Reduced hearing or visual functions.
▶ A milky film over eyes (similar to cataracts in appearance).
▶ Skin will become paler.
▶ Hallucinations.
▶ Expelling gas.
▶ May still be capable of speech.
▶ Weakness and a general lack of energy.

THE SCIENCE OF ZOMBIOLOGY
METHODS OF TRANSMISSION

Dr Ahmed studied more than 300 zombie outbreaks from the post-1945 era to the present day, plotting as accurately as possible the method of transmission of the virus to each casualty. His data confirmed that over 60% of infections are caused by zombie bites.

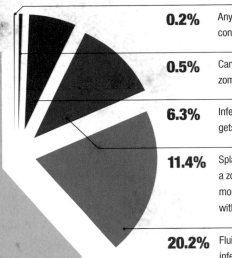

0.2% Any unnatural intimate contact with a zombie.

0.5% Cannizomb – humans eating zombies will become infected.

6.3% Infected blood or other liquid gets into food or water supply.

11.4% Splatter when hitting a zombie, exploding brain into mouth or eyes – for example with a bloater 'exploding'.

61.4% Bite from an infected human or zombie. This is by far the most common way of transmitting the zombie virus.

20.2% Fluid exchange via cuts and infected blood, for example a scratch from a zombie's nails.

3 CLINICAL DEATH
4–16 HOURS

▶ Very slow heart beat and pulse eventually ceases.
▶ Skin becomes paler, with a light blue hue in some cases.
▶ Respiration stops.
▶ All indicators point to clinical death.
▶ Body will cool quicker than a normal corpse, teeth may visibly discolor.
▶ Facebook activity will tail off.

4 ZOMBIFICATION COMPLETE
4–24 HOURS

▶ Corpse will open eyes, but breathing and heart beat will not return.
▶ Sounds include moans, groans and in some cases large discharges of trapped gas.
▶ Movement will be lumbering and slower than normal.
▶ No spoken words.
▶ The newly created zombie will attempt to consume human flesh at the first opportunity.

Dr Ahmed's Four Stages of Transformation are a generalized guideline for zombification.

THE SCIENCE OF ZOMBIOLOGY

RESEARCH IN A CRISIS

Just because you don't have any formal medical research training, doesn't mean you can't discover a cure and save the world. Science owes much to the gifted amateur.

Before toying with an apocalyptic virus try to do at least some background reading. Learn about the equipment in your lab and brush up on your basic chemistry and biology. Nothing beats learning on the job so you'll soon find out the difference between a homogenizer and a cryogenic storage container.

Small things like wearing a white lab coat and keeping strange hours can all help to get you 'in the mood' for research and don't be disappointed if you only manage to repeat that burning magnesium experience you remember from chemistry at school.

FACTS ABOUT THE VIRUS

▶ Virus particles are only about one-millionth of an inch (17 to 300 nanometers) long so special equipment will certainly be in order.

▶ Unlike human cells or bacteria, viruses carry only one or two enzymes that contain their genetic code. These enzymes are the 'instructions' for the transformation to the zombic condition.

▶ Viruses need a host cell. No cell, no zombie.

▶ The immune system in humans is totally overwhelmed by the zombie virus as it multiplies in the body. Extra doses of vitamin C and echinacea will not help patients.

▶ Antibiotics have no effect on a virus. They impact only on the reproduction of bacteria.

▶ MICROBIOLOGY 101

For those with the right skills and enthusiasm, searching for a cure to the 'zombie plague' could be a satisfying and potentially world-saving way to see out the zombie apocalypse. As your fellow survivors are battling dead across broken cities, you could be safely tucked away in a secret bunker, working on a cure and any other projects. You will still be playing a role in defeating the walking dead, albeit one away from any frontline action and horror. If you are not a trained virologist or research scientist then you need to get up to speed quickly on the fundamentals of curing an RNA virus. Try to learn what terms like lipid membrane and nucleic acid mean before the dead rise or you will be in for some serious cramming. The diagram below shows how the zombie virus enters and takes over a cell.

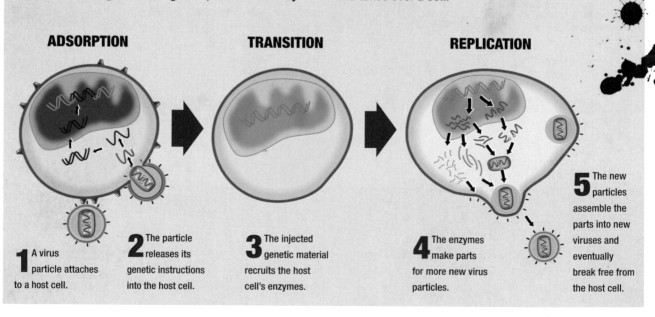

ADSORPTION

TRANSITION

REPLICATION

1 A virus particle attaches to a host cell.

2 The particle releases its genetic instructions into the host cell.

3 The injected genetic material recruits the host cell's enzymes.

4 The enzymes make parts for more new virus particles.

5 The new particles assemble the parts into new viruses and eventually break free from the host cell.

ZOMBIC MUTATIONS

The 'standard' dead are remorseless enough. They won't stop trying to feast on the flesh of the living, but the well-prepared zombie survivalist needs to be ready for any number of mutated and freakish creations which may surface during the zombie apocalypse.

COULD THE VIRUS MUTATE?

Viruses mutate; Fact. In 2008 over 100 people died when a mutated influenza strain of swine flu spread to humans. This ability to mutate and jump species makes some viruses virtually impossible to 'cure' in the traditional sense.

Remember, the only way the zombie virus can survive is through a host cell and, as we have accounts of zombism dating back thousands of years, it is likely that the virus has mutated many times over as the host immune system develops.

So, after all this science, could the zombie virus actually mutate? Answer: in all likelihood, it already has and continues to do so. Zombie survivalists have to be ever vigilant in identifying new symptoms or species jumps.

SUPERFAST ZOMBIES

The British horror film *28 Days Later* effectively reinvented the zombie for the twenty-first century. Gone were the shambling blue-grey walking corpses of George Romero orthodoxy. In their place we find the rebranded superfast and super violent zombie now renamed as 'the infected'. It made for a wonderful film and some decent sequels. However, in the field of zombiology, the film is much maligned for spreading misinformation across the zombie-fighting community. Sure the infected were an exciting fictional creation, but this is all they are. Zombies that have recently turned can almost match human running speeds, but over time they will slow down as the zombic condition develops. Here are a few more zombie myths that need to be quashed.

▶ You are unlikely to wake up in a hospital, only to find the world taken over by the dead. Chances are you will have been feasted upon long ago.

▶ Zombies do not run like Olympic athletes. Don't underestimate them but equally don't turn them into superhuman creatures.

▶ Be cautious of works of fiction when preparing for the zombie apocalypse. Some are worthy survival efforts, offering almost case-study-like accuracy. Others are pure entertainment and could lead to you preparing for a threat you will never face.

▶ MUTATION AHEAD

SIGNS TO LOOK OUT FOR

If the *X-Men* have taught us anything, it's that mutation can be both a good and a bad thing. For example, maybe the living will develop an immunity to the zombie virus or maybe the dead will lose their appetite. On the less positive side, there are five key areas you should monitor for any 'strange developments' which may indicate that the zombie virus has mutated.

 ENHANCED MENTAL CAPABILITIES

Zombies have started to think or show problem-solving ability. You notice zombies gathered in a huddle, discussing plans to attack. You notice organization in their attacks, with some creatures hanging back rather than surging forward to join the potential meat-fest.

 ENHANCED PHYSICAL CAPABILITIES

Your survival vehicle is overtaken by a running zombie with a distinct cockney accent. The dead start to seriously tear into your strong wooden door with their bloody fists. Powerful shots to the chest don't even knock a zombie down, it just continues surging on towards you.

 ENHANCED SENSES

You find you just can't shake off a zombie horde following you. No matter where you hide the dead develop an uncanny knack of finding you. You see the dead scanning buildings for any evidence of the living.

 CLASSIC MUTATIONS

Not hard to spot, you'll see creatures unknown to God walking down the road. Any humanoid with multiple heads would be a good indicator.

 VIRUS CARRIERS

Some humans may be bitten but not develop the symptoms. Look out for survivors who have prominent bite marks on their body and yet show no sign of fever or transformation. Be aware that these individuals may still be able to transfer the virus.

THE SCIENCE OF ZOMBIOLOGY

BUILDING A SECRET LAB

Planning regulations in most countries make building a secret underground laboratory or indeed any kind of 'lair' perilously difficult. Here are the key factors you will need to consider.

▶ Location is everything. No need to buy in a central location but the geology and foundations must be right. Out-of-town and wilderness sites are ideal but may prove expensive in terms of building costs.

▶ Get expert help. Building a research bunker isn't a do-it-yourself job. There are some off-the-shelf plans available, but you will need a specialist architect and scientific advisor.

▶ Hire a building project manager that is 'on the edge'. They'll need contacts in the security industry to get the kind of kit you are going to need. They should have experience in developing top-secret projects.

▶ Try to keep neighbors and casual observers in the dark. Tell them you are building a large swimming pool or a studio for your new potter's wheel. Use screens to shield sensitive work from prying eyes.

▶ THE ULTIMATE SECRET LAB

GETTING FUNDING
To build a fully equipped secret scientific research lab, it is estimated that you will need $1–2 billion. Here are some fundraising schemes you may want to consider:

▶ **START A CHARITY** Start an anti-zombie 'save the world' charity. Get celebrities involved as they normally love this kind of thing.

▶ **CHRISTMAS SINGLE** Release a classic Christmas single. Again, remember the celebrities.

▶ **CRIME PAYS** Start a secret life of crime, amassing substantial amounts of cash.

▶ **LOOK EAST** Make contact with royal families in the Middle East, explain what you're up to and that you need a large loan.

▶ **FAMILY 'INVESTMENT'** Talk to your family. They may not understand your work, but you can always brand it as an 'investment' – technically, that's not a lie.

WORKING WITH THE DEAD
At some point during your work with the virus, you will need to collect and manage 'live' zombie specimens. Working with zombies is always a dangerous activity so ensure that you keep them sealed off where possible. Always fully destroy your test subjects and wear protective clothing when conducting experiments, including safety goggles. Never assume a zombie is dormant. Always approach them with caution.

1 Large stack of comic books.
2 Full research library with leather sofa for snoozing.
3 Well-equipped research lab.
4 Defensive automated machine gun turrets.
5 Luxury sleeping quarters.
6 Stylish communal kitchen area.
7 Automated food and drink machines.
8 Supplies for at least a decade.
9 An outside door you can open to trap zombies and other specimens.
10 Containment cells for your freakish creations.
11 A white lab coat storage area.
12 Test tube and other medical supplies area.

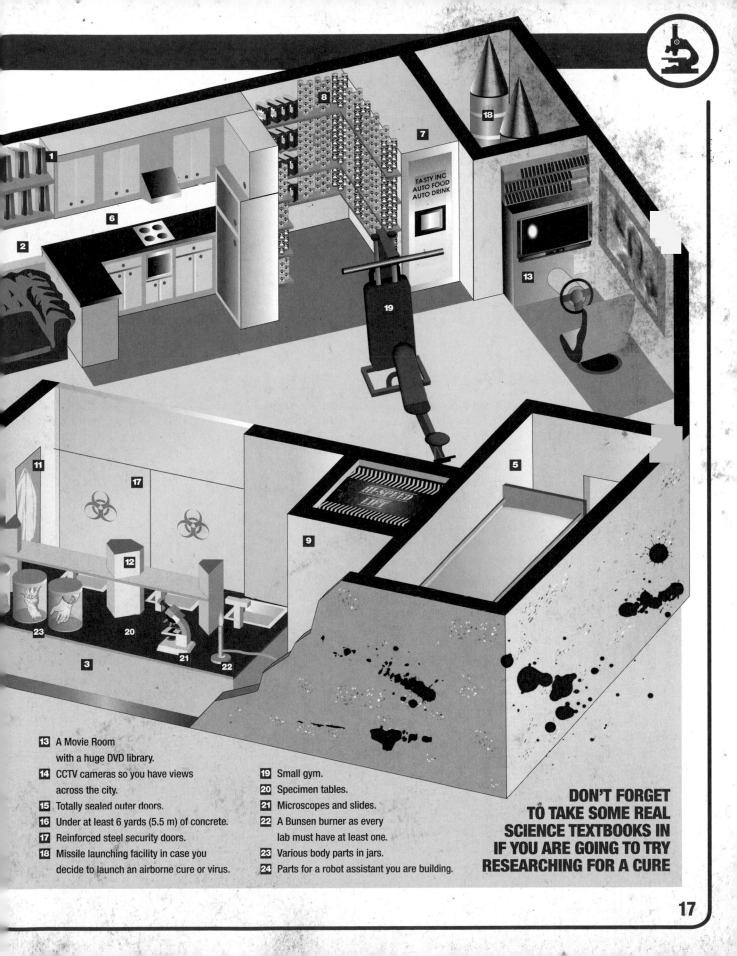

13 A Movie Room
with a huge DVD library.

14 CCTV cameras so you have views
across the city.

15 Totally sealed outer doors.

16 Under at least 6 yards (5.5 m) of concrete.

17 Reinforced steel security doors.

18 Missile launching facility in case you
decide to launch an airborne cure or virus.

19 Small gym.

20 Specimen tables.

21 Microscopes and slides.

22 A Bunsen burner as every
lab must have at least one.

23 Various body parts in jars.

24 Parts for a robot assistant you are building.

**DON'T FORGET
TO TAKE SOME REAL
SCIENCE TEXTBOOKS IN
IF YOU ARE GOING TO TRY
RESEARCHING FOR A CURE**

THE SCIENCE OF ZOMBIOLOGY

THE ZOMBIE VIRUS AND ANIMALS

To the best of our knowledge, no animal has yet developed the zombic condition. So, for now, your pets are safe from the virus. In addition, humans with the fully developed zombic condition show little interest in non-human sources of food. In outbreaks, it has often been noted that dogs and cats can walk freely through crowds of the dead without attracting any ghoulish attention.

▶ Prepare your pet for the zombie apocalypse in the same way you would any other member of the family. Create a small Bug-Out Bag containing emergency food, chew toy and any other essentials.

▶ Keep all inoculations up to date. Do not allow your pet to become overweight and maintain a healthy diet for them.

▶ Dogs in particular can be invaluable companions during the zombie crisis. Hamsters and Guinea pigs are of less use, maybe except as decoys to distract the undead.

▶ The bovine variant of the virus has been identified as a potential source of a cure for the condition in humans so don't kill cows unless you are really desperate for a steak.

REMEMBER, WILD AND STRAY DOGS WILL BECOME A MENACE AS SOCIETY FALLS APART AND RABIES WILL ALSO BE A RISK

▶ THE MOST FEARED LIST

Developing a list of the most feared 'zombie creatures' is a regular pastime in most zombie apocalypse forums across the web. While it is largely recognized that the virus does not currently transform animals or insects, zombie survivalists are a cautious crew and have prepared a list of the most deadly infected animals and insects as well as some approaches to dealing with them.

Other creatures that made the list include obvious zombie cats and dogs in common urban areas. Whereas infected chimps and orangutans will be less of a problem outside zoos and parts of the world where they still exist in the wild.

If you are engaged in any research, do not test on animals. Not only is it cruel, there is also a chance that you may stumble upon a mutated virus and cause all kinds of problems for other survivors. If you do need 'live' test subjects then you will need to develop a canny ruse to lure them into your lair. The Ministry of Zombies does not sanction any testing on humans, but if you are desperate, you can always use your lab assistant – it's what they're for.

CURRENTLY, THERE ARE NO CONFIRMED CASES OF ANIMALS, BIRDS OR INSECTS CONTRACTING THE ZOMBIC CONDITION OR TRANSFERRING THE INFECTION

MOST FEARED
THE Z-SHARK

The Z-Shark is the top of most lists. Take one of the world's most highly developed hunters, make it pretty much invincible and give all breeds an even greater taste for human flesh. Few would go near the water with such killers on the prowl. However, in reality the zombie virus could dull a shark's keen sense of smell and taste. It could have serious issues with direction and some experts picture the mentally-reduced creatures just floating to the surface, unable to function. Let's hope we never have to find out.

THE SCIENCE OF ZOMBIOLOGY
THE RISK OF ANIMAL MUTATION

The zombie virus is an incredibly complex and adaptable RNA virus and there is every possibility that it could one day mutate and affect animals. In tests, it has been shown that pets from outbreak areas are actually carrying the virus in their blood but for some reason do not develop the zombic condition which blights humans. For example, studies of an outbreak in Aleppo in Syria during the 1990s revealed that over 90% of cats and dogs in the city carried the virus in their blood and yet there were no reports of any infected pets or animals. In a post-apocalyptic world, it is best to keep clear of any stray animals and avoid the risk of infections such as rabies.

RUSSIANS AND AN INFECTED CHIMP

In 2008, documents were posted across the web reporting that Russian scientists working on a cure for the zombie virus had successfully infected a primate with the zombic condition. If true, this would be the first documented case of an animal developing and turning zombic. Some grainy photos of the primate have been leaked and can be seen on the internet, but in blurry black and white it's hard to make anything out other than the outline of an ape and a banana.

> **THE MEDIA FRENZY AROUND THE ANTI-VIRAL NATALIA_739 IS AT BEST SPECULATION AND AT WORST MISLEADING JOURNALISM. THERE IS CURRENTLY NO EVIDENCE THAT ANIMALS CAN BE INFECTED WITH THE ZOMBIE VIRUS.**

KIND OF FEARED
ZOMBIE RATS OR ZATS

Imagine their tiny feet scurrying around, overrunning every town and city. See hundreds of infected red eyes watching you from the shadows and emerging to munch on your toes as you sleep. With their numbers and size, infected rodents could become a serious threat to survivor communities. They are unlikely to be distracted by a cube of cheese (unless it's blood-soaked) and will be fiendish to kill. The one consolation again is that the zombie condition will slow them down and reduce their well-known cunning.

STILL FEARED
ZOMBIE MOSQUITOES

Forget anything large; if these zombic flyers stick their diseased proboscis into your flesh and transmit the virus directly into your blood stream, it's curtains for everyone. Many areas of the world are infested with these insects, or similar biting fiends, and you will need more than bug spray to eliminate them. In addition, with the collapse of civilization and drainage, flooding may create new habitats for this potentially deadly foe. However, in all probability it is thought that a viral jump into insects is the least likely scientific outcome – probably.

ZOMBIES IN HISTORY

The most common question asked by those sceptical about the walking dead is why there are not accounts of zombie outbreaks in history? After all, if the zombie virus has been with us for thousands of years, why aren't our history books peppered with accounts of the dead?

The real answer is remarkably simple. The rotting claw of the zombie touches human history at virtually every key point, but up to now it has rarely been acknowledged and on even fewer occasions studied. A comprehensive survey of zombic incidents has yet to be completed, but when it is, it will document outbreaks of the zombic condition from before the Ice Age.

The oldest known reference to the walking dead is in the surviving fragments of the Sumer myth-tale *The Epic of Gilgamesh* which outlines that the dead intend to 'go up to eat the living'. This is a clear reference to the cannibalistic symptoms of someone infected with the zombie virus.

Recently discovered cave paintings in the south of France show heavy-set and lumbering figures attacking fleeing cave dwellers and, in some sections, tearing and feasting on the limbs of the living. Some human-like figures can clearly be seen battling the dead, but the overall feel is one of terror, with the living scattering to escape the hungry corpses. As for the zombies themselves, they are almost stylized caricatures of the dead, painted with arms out front and typically oversized in comparison to their human prey.

ZOMBIE TIMELINE

In 2009, a pioneering group of zombie experts and academics met at Oxford University for a three-day conference on zombies in history. The outcome of one of the study groups was the world's first timeline of zombie incidents across the history of civilization. Those familiar with zombie history will immediately note the absence of several key episodes such as the walking dead outbreak in Essex in 1934 and the New York City plague of 1948. To be included in this official timeline, the outbreak needed to be confirmed by at least two documented sources and pass through the rigors of a historical investigation.

1064

An outbreak in the Normandy countryside sets back William, the Duke of Normandy's invasion plans almost three years as he attempts to control what he later referred to as a 'Saxon ruse'. Contemporary accounts see William employing expensive mercenaries from across Europe to deal with the incident. See the diaries of Brother Thomas of Rouen for further details.

3000 BCE

Eypytian hieroglyphics on Rameses II tombs shows lumbering figures being beheaded. Images of the 'undead' are common themes across the Middle Kingdom and several vases in the British Museum carry clear images of the walking dead.

55

Philosper Aristocles muses that there is 'something of hades' about some dead villagers. His was the first documented account of a zombie outbreak in Western history and was corroborated by Greek poet Herodicus in his *Journals of Adventure*.

797

Chinese general Wei-Lang uses infected blood to poison a rival warlord. He later employed the walking dead as an army to ravage his southern rivals and create one of the largest and most powerful kingdoms in China.

1576

Venetians isolate a 'zombie colony' on the cemetery island of San Michele. The site was closed to the public right up until it was razed to the ground by fire in 1933.

ZOMBIES IN HISTORY
ZOMBIE ACHIEVEMENTS

Many experienced zombie fighters will clock up literally hundreds of 'kills' as they battle their way through legions of the walking dead. Dispatching zombies will become second nature as the number dealt with rises.

However, we have already learnt that zombies are both persistent and resilient. It is easy for fighters to start underestimating their opponents. Zombies have achieved incredible things in history – maybe they haven't won any medals but they are lethal killers, either in groups or solo.

ZOMBIE SPEED

In 2002, US forces in Afghanistan were attacked by what soldiers later referred to as 'running corpses'. According to official reports, the crazed individuals ran alongside moving vehicles and were clocked at over 20 miles per hour (32 km/hr).

The Ministry of Zombies debriefed several of the soldiers involved in this report and, although unconfirmed, it is believed that the climatic conditions and recent outbreak of the zombie virus in a nearby village enabled a corpse to run at an extremely fast rate. Typically the dead cannot reach these speeds, but on this occasion they would have given an Olympic sprinter a run for his money.

ZOMBIE ENDURANCE

In 2001, a number of national newspapers in South Korea reported that a 'cannibal lunatic' had crept into an apartment block in the city of Anyang. Once inside the secure building, he murdered 10 residents before being taken out by an 87-year-old grandmother, Mrs Park, who later told a local news channel of her suspicions.

Investigations by the Ministry of Zombies in South Korea have shown that the zombie in question crawled through nearly a mile (1.6 km) of drainage pipes to gain access to the block.

The energetic Mrs Park went on to establish the Just Block It foundation in 2005, which aims to raise awareness of zombie-related drainage pipe attacks. In 2010, her tireless work finally bore fruit as legislation was introduced into the South Korean lower house to limit the diameter of any new drainage pipes fitted. As a result, from 2015 onwards, all new builds in the republic will have zombie-proof water and drainage systems.

> **THAT WAS NO MAN. IT CAME UP THROUGH THE SEWER PIPES. IT DIDN'T HAVE ANY LEGS AND I KILLED IT THE ONLY WAY YOU CAN WITH THESE CREATURES. I BLUDGEONED IT OVER THE HEAD WITH MY WALKING STICK**

MRS PARK, SOUTH KOREA

1665

An outbreak of zombies in Devon, England masks the arrival of the bubonic plague and before the disease is recognized, infected corpses have reached as far as Coventry. Before its destruction in the Second World War, Coventry Cathedral contained a mass tomb known as the 'grave of lost souls'. It is said that zombies were hurled into this grave just before the plague struck the city.

1921

Famous psychologist Sigmund Freud completed his controversial work *The Importance of Ghoulies*, in which he questioned a psychological motive behind the desire of the zombie to feed on living humans. Freud was forced to release it himself as a pamphlet. Few copies now remain, but one is available for public viewing at the Library of Congress in Vienna, Austria.

2001

Dr Khalid Ahmed isolates the zombie virus for the first time and goes on to develop the first model of zombic infection. He pioneered the mapping of symptoms over time and is widely regarded as the father of zombiology.

1780

After offending a fellow noble at a court event, the well-known French dandy the Comte de Menthe was challenged to a duel. As was the convention at the time, he duly appointed a second to fight the duel and several observers noted that this man was not stopped by either a pistol ball or a rapier strike and went on to 'feast on the defeated gentlemen'.

1999

Virologist Dr Raymond Carter creates his model of zombie infection by using computers to model a global outbreak, but it is not until 2009 that Carter finally develops the comprehensive theory of meta-hordes, in which he predicts vast, swirling swarms of the dead, numbering in their tens of millions, sweeping entire countries clean of any living survivors. This theory was novelized in 2011 in the work *Meta-Horde*.

ZOMBIES IN HISTORY

HISTORICAL ACCOUNTS

As a result of the 2009 Oxford University symposium on the walking dead, historians have begun to research specific incidents in zombie history in far more depth. New discoveries in the field of zombie science have enabled them to take a fresh look at the contemporary records and uncover the truth behind some of these mysterious outbreaks. The first volume in an official zombie history is due to be published in 2015 and will be *A Zombie History of Europe*, with further volumes to follow. But for now, zombie fighters should study these accounts to learn lessons from how our ancestors battled the dead. Three of the best examples have been examined and offer insight into surviving a zombie siege, battling bloaters and advanced combat tactics.

27 BCE–476 CE
ROMAN EMPIRE

The Roman Empire encountered many threats in its long history across the ages, but none was more persistent or dangerous than outbreaks of the zombie virus.

The Romans were the first to document the symptoms of the zombic condition and suffered periodic outbreaks from 55 CE through to the last years of the empire.

In 100 CE, philosopher, mathematician and scientist Agrippa Aquila recorded the following:

'IT IS WITHOUT QUESTION THE WICKED VAPORS OF THE RIONE MONTI WHICH CAUSE THIS AFFLICTION. IT SEEMS TO PRAY ON THE DESTITUTE AND DEPRAVED. AND, IF OUR EXPERIENCE HAS TAUGHT US ANYTHING, IT IS TO STAMP OUT THESE DISEASED VERMIN WHEREVER THEY CRAWL WITHIN OUR LANDS.'

Their grasp of the science was tenuous at best, but the Romans were brutal in their treatment of any citizen or slave found to be suffering with the zombic 'affliction'. Death was the only option. Contemporary accounts talk of legionnaires brutally clearing whole quarters of the city to quell an outbreak. For the Romans, it wasn't a question of being brutal. They realized that if the zombic condition took hold of a populous area, they would be powerless to defeat it.

1923
AUSTRALIA

Rural backwater Bramwell Station in Cape York Peninsula, Australia become front-page news in 1923 after a major zombie outbreak led to the army being deployed to bring the dead under control.

One of the most famous survival accounts from this episode became known as the Siege at Macgregor's Farm and was serialized in both the *London* and *New York Times*. The events later became the subject of the 1947 book *Through War, Zombies and Depression*.

With their isolated farmstead under siege for almost a week by over 80 zombies, the courageous Macgregors dug in and defended their home with whatever weapons they had to hand. They hammered planks over every door and window and carefully managed their supplies in near-unbearable tropical heat and humidity before being finally liberated.

The plucky Miranda Macgregor went on to publish the details of the siege in her memoir some years later.

'WE SHOWED EVERYTHING WE AUSSIES ARE PROUD OF IN THAT BLOODY SIEGE. WE FOUGHT ALONG, KEPT OUR SPIRITS UP AND RELIED ON OUR OWN SUPPLIES. NEVER ONCE DID WE THINK ABOUT GIVING UP, NOT EVEN WHEN THE DEAD WERE BANGING ON EVERY WINDOW AND DOOR.'

1964
VIETNAM

It was the US Army in Vietnam that first documented what are known in zombie-fighting circles as 'bloaters'. The tropical conditions led to infected corpses swelling up to four times their original size. The resulting creatures are slow and cumbersome but are prone to spew out infected bile and innards if they are shot or punctured, making them particularly dangerous in close combat.

US ARMY'S THREE RULES FOR BATTLING BLOATERS (MILITARY DOCUMENT 1964)

1 Maintain at least 10 yards (9 m) from the infected party.

2 Do not direct fire to the bloated mid-section – go for a target head or limb shot.

3 Shoot within 5 yards (4.6 m) and you will be infected by the resulting explosion of material.

▶ ROMANS vs THE DEAD (BELLATOR MORTIS)

The Roman Empire learnt from a series of zombie outbreaks as their territory expanded and made major changes, from how they structured their army units to developing the world's first zombie public awareness campaign.

After some early defeats, the Roman military machine quickly learnt that it needed to adapt to fight such a porous and disorganized but fearless enemy. Borrowing military wisdom from their Greek neighbors, Roman legions engaged in anti-zombie operations were restructured from a fixed, heavy infantry approach into smaller and more maneuverable units. The reforms saw the basic unit of infantry reduced and new defensive strategies emerge.

I ORGANIZATION

Small, more moveable, units of five rather than the standard eight, making them far more flexible and able to respond more quickly to the movements of their dead opponents.

II DEFENSE

Heavy emphasis on defensive shield training, with units forming a complete wall to keep out the zombies. They also spent hours practicing with a long stabbing sword, which was designed to keep the dead at arms' length.

III MOVEMENT

Roman soldiers were very fit. Trained to do slow trots over 22 miles (35.4 km) called 'dead marches' to escape the dead.

IV WEAPONS

Introduction of the 'Gladius Mortus' sword of the dead – which was long and heavier than the traditional gladius.

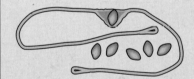

Deadly sling shot.

'A STONE TO THE HEAD, DEALS WITH THE DEAD.'

V POSTERS

Public warning posters all around Pompeii.

THE ZOMBIE APOCALYPSE

A main theme of this book is about preparing for a zombie outbreak. Most outbreaks are localized, with maybe a few hundred zombies running riot until they are dealt with. You need to have the Information and training to survive such an incident.

However, most zombie experts now agree that it is a case of when and not if the world sees a major zombie outbreak – a time when a zombie outbreak expands at an exponential rate and the number of dead soon dwarfs that of the living. This will mean the collapse of civilization, effectively the end of the humans as top of the food chain. This is a zombie apocalypse.

IF THE VIRUS HAS BEEN AROUND FOR YEARS, WHY SHOULD WE BE WORRIED ABOUT THE ZOMBIE APOCALYPSE NOW?

The world's population has grown to almost 8 billion and as the number of people increases so does the chance of a zombie outbreak. The urbanized areas have rapidly increased in the last 50 years, spawning sprawling super-cities such as Cairo, Beijing and New York. The densely packed crowds are ideal greenhouses for a major outbreak. In addition, globalization and the growth of international air travel now means that an infected individual could be half way across the world before they get the munchies.

10 REASONS TO BE WORRIED

A top entertainment and fashion magazine asked over 10,000 readers this question – why should people be concerned about zombies taking over the world?

1. Getting eaten alive would be awful.
2. Seeing a relative or close friend getting eaten wouldn't be fun.
3. Being attacked by desperate survivors or looters.
4. None of my favorite TV shows would be on.
5. I might be turned into one of the dead and I'm vegetarian so I'd get hungry.
6. My social life would dry up more than normal.
7. No Facebook – the photos may not be as nice.
8. Shops would be closed and I can't bear wearing last year's fashions.
9. I might be stuck with a group of ugly survivors.
10. There'd be no one left to read the new dystopian novel I'm writing.

MANY OF THE GENERAL PUBLIC HAVE NO UNDERSTANDING OF WHAT A ZOMBIE APOCALYPSE WOULD REALLY MEAN

ZOMBIES IN HISTORY
THINGS I WOULD DO?

In 2009 a research team conducted over 800 in-depth interviews with members of the public asking them what they'd do in the event of a zombie apocalypse.

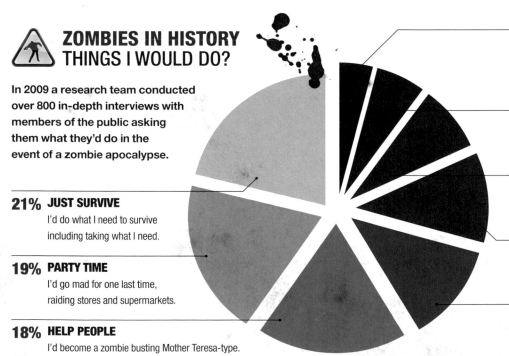

21% JUST SURVIVE
I'd do what I need to survive including taking what I need.

19% PARTY TIME
I'd go mad for one last time, raiding stores and supermarkets.

18% HELP PEOPLE
I'd become a zombie busting Mother Teresa-type.

4% SEIZE THE DAY
I like the idea of the end of the world. It'd be my chance to grab some real power.

7% BAD THINGS
I'd do bad things, very bad things – why not?

8% JOIN THE DEAD
I'd become one of the walking dead.

11% CRYOGENICS
I'd freeze myself and be defrosted in the post-apocalyptic era.

12% REVENGE
I'd start working on the people who made my list.

SURVEY VERIFIED BY THE MARKET INSIGHT GROUP

► ZOMBIE APOCALYPSE WARNING SCALE

INTERNATIONALLY RECOGNIZED SCALE

Of course not every zombie outbreak will, as they call it, 'go septic' but from our survey work, it is clear that widespread panic means you must prepare now and use a warning sign to give advance notice that the dead are on the rise. Luckily, the field of zombiology has an internationally Recognized scale of outbreaks.

CREATING YOUR OWN WARNING SCALE

- ► A few hours a week will keep you on top of developments.
- ► Build up local contacts with police, fire and ambulance services for inside information.
- ► Use informal networks of zombie spotters on the web.
- ► Have something on the wall like a whiteboard and use a traffic light system to indicate your level of alertness.

RATING	CONDITIONS AND WHAT TO EXPECT	WHAT YOU SHOULD DO?	PERSONALIZED PLAN (EXAMPLE)
Zed-Con 5 - All Clear	► Condition normal. ► The zombie virus has always been in the population but is currently latent with no reported sufferers of the zombic condition.	► Remain vigilant. ► Keep emergency supplies stocked up. ► Continue to monitor multiple new channels.	- Mrs Lowe acting strangely – zombie or just confused? - CNN article about cannibalism in France. - Will record for review later.
Zed-Con 4 Localized Outbreak	► Localized outbreak or so-called 'ghoul infestation'. ► 90% of such outbreaks are dealt with below the radar of official government. ► Most Zed-Con 4 incidents will involve fewer than one hundred zombies.	► Check in with local doctor – any extra reports of unexplained flu-like viruses? ► Check police radio for crimes involving cannibalism.	- Small outbreak in China on web – am monitoring. - Took day off school to monitor developments. - Parents canceledDisney trip. Not happy.
Zed-Con 3 Regional Outbreak	► A more significant outbreak, often involving more than one village or a small town. ► Zombie numbers are typically 1000+. ► Expect army intervention, road blocks and stories of 'industrial accidents'.	► No matter where it is in the world, prepare for lockdown. ► Keep your fellow survivors updated.	- Checked off all stocks. - Called all of survivor group. - Preparing for lockdown.
Zed-Con 2 National Outbreak	► Several cities or states are dominated by zombies. ► The country will be under martial law. ► Information will be unreliable. ► Zombie numbers are typically 10,000+.	► Last chance to check on any elderly neighbors. ► Risk foraging only if you are missing something vital.	- Full lockdown. - Emergency broadcasts report all roads closed. - Implementing 90-day plan.
Zed-Con 1 Global Pandemic	► World travel and communication breaks down. ► Governments and central authority will crumble. ► More and more countries will turn 'gray' as the zombies take over.	► Deliver strong leadership. ► Go through the 90-day survival plan again. ► Deal with any of the dead who take an interest in your home.	- This is the big one! - Re-checked all stocks. - Took out two zombies trying to get into the garden. Good to get my first kills. Me 2 Zombies 0!

BECOMING A ZOMBIE SURVIVALIST

Let's be honest here – if you are doing nothing to prepare for the zombie apocalypse, your chances of surviving more than three months in a nation overrun by the dead are extremely small – in fact, it's less than 0.005%. That's a fact.

If these facts tell us anything, it's that you'd better change your mindset and start preparing for the zombies now.

Before lurching into depression, it's worth noting that moderate changes to your lifestyle and circumstances can drastically improve your chances of survival. For example, simple factors such as keeping a Bug-Out Bag of supplies handy, keeping fit and reading up on the walking dead, can all start to decrease the likelihood of you becoming a cheap meat snack in the first few days. Your aim is to be one of the zombie survivalists to make it through. And, right here is where you have to start. You need to address four key areas to be the complete zombie survivalist.

WHAT ARE MY CHANCES OF:

1 in 25	Getting food poisoning
1 in 117	Being on plane with an incapacitated pilot
1 in 215	Dating a millionaire
1 in 2,232	Fatally slipping in a bath or shower
1 in 7,000	Being considered possessed by Satan
1 in 20,000	Surviving the zombie apocalypse without preparation
1 in 10,000,000	Dying from parts falling off an airplane
1 in 20,000,000	Odds of getting elected President of the United States
1 in 43,000,000	Being hit by a burning meteor
1 in 52,000,000	Being killed by a falling fridge

AREAS TO ADDRESS

AREA 1
MENTALITY

You must want to survive. If you can't survive without the latest slice of reality TV, you may as well give up. With the world going to hell around you, you need to be 100% convinced that you want to survive and prosper. This is known as the 'survival mentality' and you can't order it online.

AREA 2
KNOWLEDGE

You must understand the threats you face and seize any opportunities. Know your enemy, their tactics and weaknesses. Review the likely impact on your country and local area and plan accordingly. Read reliable outbreak accounts and become familiar with how things pan out when the dead come to town.

HOW TO BE 'ZOMBIE' STREET SMART

There is much you can do before the dead rise to ensure that you are mentally prepared for the challenges ahead. Any formal military, outbound or firearms training are obvious choices as are camping, cooking and gardening as key subjects that will help you survive. It's also important that you start to develop a survivor mentality – that you become Zombie Street Smart. No survival book will teach you how to be Zombie Street Smart. Sure, you can learn about the threats and look for the right signs, but true zombie awareness is about maintaining that level of vigilance at all times. Here are some pointers:

- ▶ **Know your neighborhood.** Always think about where zombies could be lurking and how to get home safely.
- ▶ **Always keep your eyes open** – never walk along listening to music or you may miss the moan of an approaching zombie.
- ▶ **Always have an escape route** – no matter where you are, at work, on the train, at the store – remember how you came in and have an alternative escape route.
- ▶ **Be on the lookout for signs of the zombic condition** – gray skin, milky eyes, feverish and with an unhealthy interest in eating the flesh of others.
- ▶ **Tell as many people as you can about the threat of the zombies.** Who knows, you might save someone's life?

As you become more zombie street smart, you will start to develop what zombie preppers refer to as a 'hyper awareness' of anything zombic. You'll find you're always watching for those tell-tale signs and start to see the walking dead around every corner.

10 SIGNS YOU ARE READY TO BE A ZOMBIE SURVIVALIST

As your training progresses and you learn new survival skills, you will acquire 'rep' or a reputation amongst the zombie survival community. You'll find that other experts will willingly share their experience with a fellow enthusiast. However, as others find out about your curious training regime, some at work or school may begin to treat you as a bit of a 'nut' or 'weirdo'. Do not let this put you off – you'll have the last laugh when these individuals are being mauled by zombies and you are safely barricaded in at home.

1. You have become known at work as the 'zombie guy or gal'.
2. You're actually quite looking forward to it all kicking off so you can try out your kit.
3. Work colleagues see flu, you see possible zombie virus when someone turns up at work with a slight fever.
4. When booking holidays, you think carefully about the impact if you are caught abroad.
5. You spend more than two hours a week on your homemade zombie monitoring graph.
6. You have mini Bug-Out Bags to take to school.
7. You think of *Dawn of the Dead* as a training video.
8. You scan the TV channels for anything zombie related.
9. You had a serious discussion with a friend in which you tried to convince them about the threat.
10. When in the DIY center, you see possibilities everywhere for ramping up your home defenses.

AREA 3
TRAINING

Knowledge must be supported by practical experience. Obviously, it may be hard for you to find zombies to practice your fighting skills on, but there are plenty of outdoor survival, first aid and gardening courses available for you to acquire invaluable experience before the dead turn up.

AREA 4
AWARENESS

You must have a monitoring system up and running at all times. Monitor the news channels, the internet and stay in touch with fellow zombie survivalists to keep an eye on events around the world. People you may once have considered 'nuts' may become some of your best friends as you make your way through the 'zombie preppers' world.

BECOMING A ZOMBIE SURVIVALIST

GETTING THE LOOK

Never forget that you will not be able to flick a switch and suddenly become a zombie survivalist when the zombies arrive – we are talking about a mentality here – you must live and breathe zombie survival. This may involve some real changes in your lifestyle and certainly your wardrobe. The Ministry of Zombies advises a three-step approach to get this right:

▶ **BECOMING A HARD GUY OR GAL**
▶ **THE ZOMBIE SURVIVALIST LOOK**
  – PRE-APOCALYPSE
▶ **THE ZOMBIE SURVIVALIST LOOK**
  – ONCE THE OUTBREAK BEGINS!

▶ BECOMING A HARD GUY OR GAL

Surviving the zombies is not just about fighting the dead, it's about being able to look after yourself, so developing a new tough as nails personality now is a great way to start. Here are six ways you can get that 'hard' look:

1 Do scary things like rapelling and show no fear about anything. Never admit to being afraid of heights or spiders. You need to become known as a fearless type, with a little of the loose cannon about you.

2 Use a 'hard man' walk whether you are male or female – that confident swagger will ensure that all will take notice.

3 Use silence skilfully. Don't talk too much and never ask for help. When you do talk, use short and slightly mysterious sentences, hinting that you have seen a lot but don't want to talk about it.

4 Use every opportunity to reinforce the general perception that you are tough – for example, never complain of a headache or toothache. Throw in the occasional phrase like – 'I think I broke a rib this morning at my full contact kickboxing class.' Then wait for the shock response and reply coolly, 'It's not the first time.'

5 Don't start fights but if you are in action, make sure you are the one who finishes it.

6 Use every opportunity to show what a hard nut you are by helping others and playing the knight in shining armor, but look cool while doing it. Rarely smile.

These top tips can help you build a 'tough' persona and, when combined with your strict training regime, it will not be long before you develop what is known as a 'Rambo personality'.

▶ THE ZOMBIE SURVIVALIST LOOK

PRE-APOCALYPSE

In most countries, it's just not possible to live every day looking like an extra from a *Mad Max* movie. However, you should support your new persona with a tough as nails look. Here are five pointers on how to dress:

1. Boots always work so wear them; black combat boots can give you that tough edge.
2. Tear the sleeves off your shirt and wear jeans with rips and holes in them. Never button a shirt all the way up.
3. Try a worn-out black leather jacket and combat or cargo pants combo – never wear a skirt (unless you're a Scotsman) – particularly if you are male.
4. Sport a mean and intimidating look on your face to go with the outfit. Practice this in the mirror to avoid looking as if you are unwell or have indigestion.
5. Finally, get the hair right – generally styles which require a hairdryer will not help. If you are female, you must avoid looking like Tina Turner in *Mad Max Beyond Thunderdome*.

ONCE THE OUTBREAK BEGINS!

Once the outbreak starts, it's time to put all of your training and preparation into action. You can now change into your full zombie apocalypse outfit, including weapons and accessories. Armed with these and your new hard persona you will drastically increase your chances of surviving.

▶ Stylish headband.
▶ Steel toe caps.
▶ Decent walking boots.
▶ Tough haircut.
▶ Cool shades.
▶ A perfected mean stance.
▶ Adorned in weapons.
▶ A light pack for supplies and any loot.
▶ Leather jacket with studs.
▶ Optional severed zombies ears for extra 'hardness' appeal.
▶ Must have the right name – not Kevin or Dave.
▶ Walking the delicate line between hard case and parody.
▶ Good belt with useful accessory compartments.
▶ A mean stare which says 'don't mess with me'.
▶ Post-apoc dog companion optional.

THINK TOUGH, LOOK TOUGH AND STAY TOUGH!

BECOMING A ZOMBIE SURVIVALIST

BE READY OR BE DEAD!

The Bug-Out Bag is a feature of every good survival guide but the Ministry of Zombies has pioneered the creation of an entire system to help you and your family survive a zombie apocalypse.

The Bug-Out System is an emergency set of procedures to ensure that you make the best possible start when the dead rise. It consists of three main elements.

► **BUG-OUT BAG**
► **BUG-OUT LOCATION**
► **BUG-OUT PLAN**

In essence, the Bug-Out Bag should contain emergency supplies to get you through the first 24–48 hours of any zombie crisis. Your Bug-Out Locations are either safe houses or bolt holes you can reach in case you get caught away from your main secure location. Your Bug-Out Plan draws the two parts above together in a maintenance schedule for the Plan together with any maps, guides or routes you have planned. If you are already at home, it should be in an easy-to-reach location. If your home base is overrun, it's what you grab when you 'bug out'.

► CREATING A BUG-OUT BAG

The purpose of a Bug-Out Bag is to provide you with the tools and resources to make it through the first 48 hours. It is a common mistake that newly trained zombie survivalists often make to overload their bags, packing them full of everything from extra ammunition to some light reading to help make any periods in hiding bearable. Let's be clear: over packing your Bug-Out Bag will get you killed. If it significantly slows you down or hampers your movement, the statistics show that you are far more likely to be eaten by the dead.

'STAY LIGHT, STAY MOBILE AND STAY ALIVE'

Here are the suggested contents for a typical 'at work' Bug-Out Bag. This is something office workers can easily carry on their daily commutes.

⚠ LEGAL ADVICE

THE CONTENTS OF YOUR BUG-OUT BAG MUST MEET ANY LEGAL REQUIREMENTS IN YOUR COUNTRY. CARRYING AN INAPPROPRIATE COCKTAIL OF PETROL BOMBS AND OTHER WEAPONS IS NOT ADVISED WHERE LOCAL LAWS DO NOT ALLOW.

BECOMING A ZOMBIE SURVIVALIST
ADVICE FOR THOSE WITH DISABILITIES

Preparation is vital for anyone looking to survive in a land of the dead, but there are some additional challenges for those with disabilities. For example, your Bug-Out Plan, and indeed all survival planning, will need to take into account any special medical or physical requirements.

In terms of Bug-Out preparation, it is recommended that any bag must be light enough to carry easily. So if you have to take out some contents, simply trim down the list or look for lighter alternatives. Equally, aids such as a wheelchair or walking stick may present useful opportunities to conceal a weapon in clear view.

The Ministry of Zombies advises against using any internationally recognized signals for help, such as a white blanket hung from the window. There will be many desperate people out there ready to take advantage of a carefully prepared survivor.

With the right preparation, those with disabilities have very much the same chance as others to make it through the zombie apocalypse. The important thing is to complete a thorough needs assessment and then ensure that any resulting recommendations are integrated with your survival plan.

BOLT HOLE LOCATIONS

1 WATER BOTTLE OR FLASK
At least 17 oz (500 ml). Use sparingly and be cautious of other sources.

2 COMPASS AND LOCAL MAP
With plotted escape routes – know this document well.

3 LOCATION OF ANY BOLT HOLES
Easy to forget in a panic (in code if required).

4 A GOOD FLASHLIGHT
The electricity may not last long so be prepared for the dark.

5 FULLY PACKED WATERPROOFS
Particularly in areas where cold will be an issue.

6 A SMALL FIRST AID KIT
Important to keep any cuts or grazes away from infected blood.

7 FISHING WIRE
A thousand uses such as zombie trip wires. Also very light.

8 PROTEIN OR CHOCOLATE BARS
Instant energy and calories are what's required.

9 ICE CLIMBER AXE
Any questions and you can explain it's a new hobby.

10 A SMALL BLANKET
Do not use the modern silver 'space blankets' as the noise will attract the dead.

11 A BOTTLE OF COLOGNE OR AFTERSHAVE
This odd item could save your life.

BECOMING A ZOMBIE SURVIVALIST

▶ BUG-OUT LOCATIONS

Bug-Out Location typically refers to a secondary site you and your survivor group can relocate to if your primary location is overrun. But it also refers to any pre-checked 'safe' site you have scoped out.

LOCATIONS TO AVOID

During a major zombie outbreak, chaos and destruction will fill towns and cities. Hundreds of thousands of civilians will be unprepared when the walking dead stagger into view. It is estimated by the Ministry of Zombies that law and order as we know it will break down in most urban areas within 72 hours. With this in mind, some locations should certainly be ruled out as safe places to hide from the zombies.

 PLACE OF WORSHIP

A shelter in times of trouble for many, a veritable buffet feast for the zombies. Expect carnage as church or temple goers rush to these sites.

 HOSPITALS AND CLINICS

The front line of war against a virus. Unfortunately, with the zombie virus it's a war we've already lost. Avoid like the plague and expect these sites to be overrun with fresh zombies as people are brought in with the zombic condition already developing.

 AIRPORTS AND DOCKS

Take rush hour and multiply it a hundred times, then add in thousands of infected. Trying to catch a plane or boat to safety will be almost impossible after the first hours of the crisis. Most zombie survivalists assume that long-distance travel of any kind will be impossible.

CAUGHT ABROAD?

Most travel insurance companies will regard zombie attacks as 'acts of nature' and such events are therefore largely excluded from most policies. If, however, you are on holiday, or away on business, during a zombie incident, the current guideline is to barricade yourself in either your hotel room or a nearby friendly embassy.

Do not attempt to reach an airport or railway station. Expect roads to be gridlocked. It is advisable that you learn 'I'm not one of them' in the relevant language.

COMMUNICATION CARDS

The Ministry of Zombies has developed a set of cards, which can be used to communicate in a zombie crisis in any country. They are available in various sizes and can be used if you are stranded in a country and have little grasp of the local language. If you are caught in this situation, do not panic; just slowly hold your card up. Zombie fighting groups around the world have been trained to recognize these symbols.

▶ **ZOMBIES ARE COMING!**
▶ **I'M NOT A ZOMBIE!**
▶ **LET'S JOIN TOGETHER AND FIGHT ZOMBIES**

ZOMBIE SUPPORT CARD

ZOMBIES ARE COMING!

ZOMBIE SUPPORT CARD

I'M NOT A ZOMBIE!

ZOMBIE SUPPORT CARD

JOIN TOGETHER AND FIGHT

► BUG-OUT PLAN

Your Bug-Out Plan should include a list of well-scouted locations to cover your immediate area and routes. Walk your target routes slowly, checking for any potential hazards and making notes of any safe bolt holes you may be able to use. Remember that during the zombie apocalypse your route is likely to be heaving with panicky crowds and even looters.

▶ Prepare your own Bug-Out Bag. You may have a version to keep at work or in the car.
▶ Assess the needs of the family and friends you plan to survive with (if any).
▶ Secure your home location. See the 90-Day Survival Plan from the Ministry of Zombies.
▶ Identify at least three routes back to your home location from your place of work and any other sites you frequent. Print and laminate routes if necessary and know them by heart.
▶ Target several 'bolt holes' along your routes to ensure that you have a temporary location should the situation on the ground prove 'too hot'. Typical examples would include hidden drainage ditches, empty homes or copses of trees.
▶ Take the time to build a list of at least two 'alpha sites'. These are locations which you have scouted and should be known to all members of your group. If you are overrun, this is where you meet up. They can be anything from a secure lock-up garage complete with spare supplies and weapons, to a well-known wood in which your scattered party can regroup in the trees.

DON'T BECOME A CHEAP MEAT SNACK FOR THE ZOMBIES. PREPARE NOW!

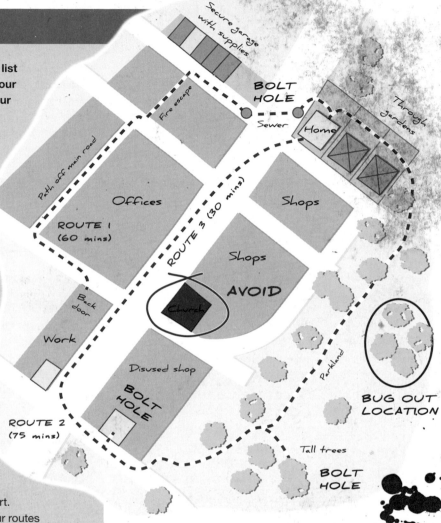

ZOMBIE PREPAREDNESS JOURNAL

This is one of the best ways to keep you on track with your zombie survival plans. Set yourself some achievable objectives and make an effort to do something 'zombie' every day – be it exercise, learning or checking your supplies.

▶ Start with scheduling an exercise program and then noting your times and achievements each day.
▶ Arrange to stock up with a few extra items on shopping day and track your supplies.
▶ Schedule a weapons training hour every week and stick to it. Give yourself a reward if you complete five sessions.
▶ Ensure that you have a time each week when you revisit your survival plan. It may be daunting at the start, but pick up tasks every week and keep working through them.

ANTI-ZOMBIE PRODUCTS

There has been an explosion in the range of products on the market which profess to either 'cure' the zombic condition or 'scare' off the walking dead. The Ministry of Zombies, working with *What! Magazine,* has investigated many of these products and most have proven ineffective at best, and dangerous at worst.

To date, these investigations have ensured that over 300 products were removed from public sale. The most high-profile product taken off the virtual shelf being the now notorious range of Banjo Brand anti-ghoul merchandise, which flooded the market in 2009 and included all manner of creams, potions and tonics professing to help the unwary defend themselves against the dead. However, the battle goes on and new products seem to be emerging every week.

The market for anti-zombie products is not regulated by any international body as the items fall outside legislation on medicines for human usage and standard consumer products. Here are the worst offenders.

▶ MONROE'S ZOMBIE PELLETS

Simply spread the small brown pellets around your property, adding more as required at any point where the dead gather. The creatures will be drawn by the meaty scent of the pellets and consume them. But at Monroe's, we care too much to hurt these misguided souls. Once they have consumed our pellets, the dead will drift away – their desire for living flesh gone. A humane solution to a human problem.

'A SAFE AND HUMANE WAY TO ENSURE YOUR HOME STAYS FREE OF THE DEAD.'

PRODUCT REVIEW 👍👍👍👍👍

An expensive and useless product. We found these pellets to be a mixture of sawdust and glue. They have no effect on the dead but did attract significant numbers of slugs and snails. In addition, cats and dogs seem to find these dry pellets irresistible and suffer from the unpleasant side effect of acute trapped wind.

▶ BITE-AWAY

Using the latest research, Bite-Away cream will cure bites and scratches from any of the infected. Apply liberally to the affected area, slowly massaging the cooling cream into the wound. Within hours, the healing process will begin and you will be completely virus-free within 24 hours. If dizziness or moaning occurs, this may be a side effect or you could be turning into a zombie. Please consult your medical professional before use.

'THE WORLD'S FIRST ANTI-BACTERIAL VIRUS CREAM SPECIALLY FORMULATED TO HEAL THOSE IRRITATING ZOMBIE BITES!'

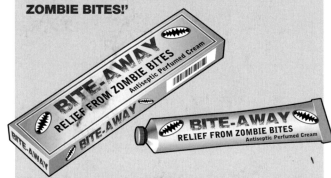

PRODUCT REVIEW 👍👍👍👍👍

This is a scandalous product, which is sold on multiple sites across the internet. Tests have shown that it contains no active ingredients and derives from cream for treating rashes. Don't trust it, don't buy it. If you get bitten and use it, then you deserve what you get – you have been warned!

UNCLE TED'S ANTI-GHOUL TONIC

'SOMETIMES THE OLD WAYS ARE THE BEST AND OLD UNCLE TED KNEW HIS TONIC COULD REALLY CURE WHAT AILS YOU, SO WE JUST HAD TO GET IT TO YOU GOOD PEOPLE!'

Back in the old days Uncle Ted discovered the secret to curing the blight that brings the dead back to life. If you are feasted on by one of these unfortunates, take three table spoons of this powerful tonic and you'll wake up the next day feeling fine and dandy. Uncle Ted's Anti-Ghoul Tonic has been curing the undead for almost one hundred years. It is also available in a gallon spray can, which you can shower in.

BANJO BRAND

Banjo Brand products are notorious in the zombie fighting community for their ineffectiveness. The family making the range, which includes the dangerous Hi-Strength Healing Poultice said to 'cure' zombie bites, frequently moves between trailer parks across the United States and has so far eluded any state prosecution.

PRODUCT REVIEW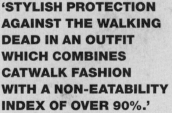

This product has been on the market for decades and is a useless home remedy load of rubbish. Tests in the Ministry laboratories showed that it was at least 12% cat's urine and contained dangerous levels of lead and alcohol. Steer clear of the Banjo Brand and any of their products.

ZOMBIE-PROOF BODY SUIT

Developed by the US Government during the Cold War, Desiree Survival Fashions now brings you the world's first complete zombie-proof range of street wear. As others cower indoors, you'll be able to wander the streets, checking out the latest fashions in safety and the dead will ignore you as if you weren't there. Available in satin white, luscious peach and new nifty pink, a Micranax suit could be what you are looking for to ensure that just because the world's falling apart, it doesn't mean your sense of fashion has to as well!

'STYLISH PROTECTION AGAINST THE WALKING DEAD IN AN OUTFIT WHICH COMBINES CATWALK FASHION WITH A NON-EATABILITY INDEX OF OVER 90%.'

PRODUCT REVIEW 👍👍👍👍

We have no words to explain how poor this suit is. It is totally ineffective at protecting against the dead and retails on eBay at over $400. It appears to be a standard bee keeper's outfit with some glitter thrown on. We wonder what kind of fool would actually go for an obvious fake like this.

BECOMING A ZOMBIE SURVIVALIST

BUILD YOUR OWN SURVIVOR TEAM

Zombie survival is all about planning, so use the chart below to help assemble a team with the right skills to stay alive when the world goes to hell. If you don't know people who fit into these roles, get out there and meet them.

The Ministry of Zombies recognizes ten distinct survival profiles which should be covered to give any group the best chance of survival. Of course, some skill sets may be covered by one individual, such as a skilful mechanic who is also adept at battling the dead. However, ensure that key skills are spread across the group. For example, everyone

will need to be able to wield a hand weapon and it will be useful if the whole team can pitch in making your home base safe. So, if necessary, audit the skills of your group and arrange training sessions to develop the skills you will need to survive. Don't panic if you don't have everything covered, but do take the time to work on any gaps.

As a final note on roles, it may be a good idea not to tell the person you have labelled 'first to die' as it may impact on their morale and ironically end up getting them killed sooner than they would otherwise have been.

TEAM LEADER

This is your role – make sure you are up to it. Start acting the part now by strutting around making 'firm but fair' decisions. With the knowledge gained from this volume, you will quickly become the 'go to' person.

GROUP MASCOT

Must be cute, chirpy and ready with a motivational phrase at all times including 'come on guys, there are only a few hundred' or 'if anything, it'll be more fun without ammunition'.

WEAPONS EXPERT

Armed with a baseball bat or crowbar, this fighter should love dealing with the dead up close and personal. They will also be responsible for ensuring that everyone else is armed and ready for combat.

THE MEDIC

A qualified doctor or nurse with the skills and first aid kit to complete everything from treating a strange rash to major surgery. Must come equipped with own bandages.

QUARTER -MASTER

This must be someone with an eye for detail and scrupulous honesty as they'll be managing the supplies. It'd be handy if they dislike many types of food as that way, your cans of peaches will be safe.

DIY GUY OR GAL

Carpentry, welding or bricklaying – this survivor must have all the skills crucial to keep your home fortress maintained. They should ideally have their own tools.

▶ STARTING A ZOMBIE NEIGHBORHOOD WATCH (ZNW)

Creating a zombie neighborhood watch group is a great way to protect your local area against the walking dead. Like a regular neighborhood watch group it will involve meetings, agreeing to a rotation of patrols and communicating with your local law enforcement agencies.

You can begin the process with a friendly letter to all of your neighbors. It is often useful to include the phrase 'Have you ever worried about how you would cope if the zombies attacked our quiet road?' You'll be surprised how many people haven't given it a lot of thought.

Set a date for a 'kick off' meeting and start getting organized. On the agenda should be an audit of the skills you have within the group, a discussion of your defensive plans as well as an educational session using the content from this volume. Feel free to photocopy the pages you need for any neighborhood watch work. Finally, it may be an idea to produce anti-zombie hats and stickers to help give a community feel to the whole venture. You can then sit back and watch the price of local homes soar as word gets out that your neighborhood is 'zombie prepared'.

MECHANIC GUY OR GAL

You'll always need one of these to ensure that your post-apocalyptic wheels are kept running. Ideally, they should get along with your DIY person as they will often have to team up. Select someone who comes with their own tools.

EX-SPECIAL FORCES

It is always useful to have your own armed and trained killer. This survivor will become your right hand and you need to be able to rely on them to report back on any potential trouble within the group. You may even end up needing them to 'solve a problem' for you.

FIRST TO DIE

A tough slot to fill but if the old series of *Star Trek* taught us anything, it is that you must always have one of those guys in the red security shirts as they invariably die first. Do not reveal to this person that they fulfil this role.

DAZED AND CONFUSED

There must alway be someone in your group who is in a state of denial about the dead or raving on the edge about the 'world that's gone'. They will use phrases such as 'we're all gonna die!' and 'game over man, game over!'.

GROUP LAWYER

It is important to always have adequate legal representation – only joking. Leave them outside. Some professions which demand vast salaries now will be worthless in the world of the zombies. It's very sad but true.

ZOMBIE SURVIVAL EXAM

ZOMBIE SURVIVAL
BASIC LEVEL

This paper has been approved by the Ministry of Zombies in London and the State Department for Defense against the Walking Dead in Washington DC. Citizens are encouraged to undertake this examination and are awarded a Basic Level in Zombie Survival upon successful completion.

INSTRUCTIONS TO CANDIDATE

▶ You should attempt all questions on the paper.
▶ You must base your answers on the content of this manual.
▶ For the 20 questions, you should score 15 or above to pass.
▶ 10 minutes. This is a closed-book examination.

1 Which of the following are warning signs of the zombie apocalypse?

A The media is full of reports of 'unexplained cannibalism'.
B My supermarket has a two-for-one offer on avocados.
C Re-runs of *Dawn of the Dead* on television.
D You had a nightmare about zombies.

2 How do you 'kill' a zombie?

A Threaten it verbally.
B Chase it away and it will die of hunger.
C A stake through the heart.
D Smash at least 80% of the brain.

3 Which of the following causes the development of the zombic condition?

A Voodoo.
B Being in a cemetery at night.
C The zombie RNA virus.
D Radiation.

4 One of the most important features of zombie home defense is:

A A nice glass conservatory.
B A white picket fence.
C A landscaped garden with delightful water feature.
D Double- or triple-glazing on all windows and doors.

5 Which of the following is a good zombie survival location?

A A hospital – they're bound to have a cure.
B A Church – it's bound to be safe there.
C A big tent in the middle of the park.
D A fortified and fully supplied home.

6 Which of the following is a component of any Bug-Out Bag?

A Essential food and water for 24 hours.
B The latest copy of *Vogue*.
C A TV Guide.
D Your priceless collection of *Star Trek* figurines.

7 Your granny has been bitten by a zombie. What do you do?

A Forget about it, it's only a scratch.
B Get her started on some antibiotics.
C Qietly get the hammer.
D Try to cleanse and bind the wound.

8 Which of the following is a better weapon to fight zombies with?

A An empty gun – it might scare them off.
B A metal baseball bat – ideal for bashing brains.
C A rapier sword – for striking with precision at the heart.
D A small fruit peeler from IKEA.

9 Which scientist is known as the 'father' of zombiology?

A Dr Khalid Ahmed.
B Dr Spock.
C Dr Beverly Crusher.
D Dr No.

10 Why should you watch plenty of approved zombie films?

A Because they are a great substitute for any real training.
B Because I believe everything on TV.
C Because they may present some realistic survival scenarios to learn from.
D I don't have anything else to do.

11 Do you believe that zombies should have human rights?

A Of course, they're people too.
B No way. It's kill or be killed.
C We should offer them something.
D Sure, why not? Maybe we could all live together.

12 Your attitude to zombie survival can best be summed up by the following statement:

A No, no, no – they don't exist!
B I plan to join Team Edward.
C I want to join the undead horde, it sounds like fun.
D I'm trained, I'm prepared and I'm going to survive.

MINISTRY OF ZOMBIES

13 Which of the following is not a type of zombie?

A A classic.

B A limbless wonder.

C A double zinger with cheese.

D A snapper.

14 Which of the following is a recognized post-apocalyptic survival group?

A Barons of the Zompoc.

B Door-to-door sales people.

C The Moonies.

D Cancelled cowboy space series fans who complain endlessly.

15 Putting zombie warning posters up around my neighborhood will:

A Tell people I'm nuts.

B Encourage children to chase and throw stones at me.

C Warn people about the very real threat they face.

D Give me something to do.

16 You come across another survivor group when out foraging, do you?

A Run and hug them.

B Kill them all and run away screaming.

C Entice the zombies towards them.

D Treat them with caution, being firm but friendly until you know their motives.

17 Which of the following is not a symptom of the zombic condition?

A A slow stumbling walk.

B A desire to feast on human flesh.

C Fangs.

D A vacant gaze and no speech.

18 I would describe myself as a 'zombie survivalist' by saying:

A I mean the zombie books are okay, but vampires are cooler.

B Not really. I enjoy the films enough.

C Yeah – as a joke. They're fictional anyway.

D I would proudly describe myself as a zombie survivalist and go to explain the dangers of the walking dead to others.

19 You can safely eat zombie meat as a healthy alternative to beef:

A Indeed. It's is particularly nice with a fine mushroom sauce and sipping a good Chianti.

B You should never eat zombies – it's foul and may spread the infection.

C Why not, I'll try anything once.

D This makes sense as fresh meat will be hard to get.

20 Does the average person need to do any special preparation for the zombie apocalypse?

A No – it's best to just take it as it comes.

B No – I plan to go *Mad Max* anyway.

C Yes – I bought a lovely new set of camouflage trousers.

D Yes – people need to embark on a complete program of zombie survival preparation and training.

ANSWERS

20 D	19 B
18 D	17 C
16 D	15 C
14 A	13 C
12 D	11 B
10 C	9 A
8 B	7 C
6 A	5 D
4 D	3 C
2 D	1 A

YOUR SCORE • BASIC LEVEL

15-20 You have a good understanding of zombie apocalypse preparation and the threats these creatures face to humanity. You have achieved the level required and are awarded a Basic Certificate in Zombie Survival. Any score over 17 entitles you to a merit score.

10-14 You have clearly learned lessons from this book, but you have not quite achieved the required standard. Check back through the chapters you did not understand and then sit through the paper again.

Below 9 This is below average and most unimpressive. One wonders if you are taking this whole zombie survival thing seriously. Either go back to the start of the book and start cramming or become a quick and easy snack for the dead when they arrive.

In 2009, the Ministry of Zombies consulted with several government bodies after being asked to review the possible development of zombie survival certification for both children and adults. The project was shelved in 2012 with ministers citing 'cost concerns' as the main reason. Here at the Ministry of Zombies, we still maintain that Tahiti was the best location to review and produce our research.

Only two sample papers were created and are presented here for the first time. After thoroughly reviewing the content in this book, you should attempt to complete Paper 1 to achieve a Basic Certificate in Zombie Survival. After further study and training, you should move on to Paper 2 to achieve an Advanced Certificate in Zombie Survival.

ZOMBIE SURVIVAL EXAM

ZOMBIE SURVIVAL
ADVANCED LEVEL

Do not attempt the Advanced Level paper until you have completed your Basic Level qualification. The Advanced Level Certification provides you with a survival profile – you must score in the top two boxes to pass and achieve certification.

INSTRUCTIONS TO CANDIDATE

▶ You should attempt all questions on the paper.
▶ Your scores at the end will provide you with a 'survival profile' and supporting analysis.
▶ 10 minutes. This is a closed-book examination.

1 There is one course of action when a survivor has been infected:

A Chop, chop and chop again with an axe.
B There is no cure so isolate them and consider the end game.
C Give them paracetamol – might be flu.
D Set them free to join the rest of the zombies.

2 A group of survivors arrives and hammers on the door – they want to come in and escape from the zombies:

A Tell them to get lost, you've got the supplies but you ain't one to share
B Find out more about them, then quarantine them and have them join your group.
C Open your door and give them the help they need.
D Run outside and hug them, it's been weeks since you've seen anyone.

3 You look at your current home and decide to make some improvements. Do you?

A Take out the stairs to provide a well-defended 'green zone' on the upper floors.
B Complete a Zombie House audit and act on the outcomes.
C Consider double-glazing but it is expensive.
D Put a delightful rockery in by the pond.

4 You find an injured survivor along the road. He has clearly been bitten. Do you?

A Put him out of his misery and steal all of his supplies. He won't be needing them soon.
B Knock him out when he's not looking and then take all his supplies.
C Allow him to travel with you until he turns.
D Sit down and talk about the old days.

5 You are captured by a group of cannibals. Do you?

A Offer to bring them more human survivors if they let you go, then honor this foul pledge.
B Fight to the death, hoping to clean the earth of this sickening scum.
C Call them inbred mutants and say you will be writing a letter of complaint.
D Try to talk them round to your vegan stance.

6 You are out foraging and come face to face with another armed survivor – you are both looking at the same box of supplies. Do you?

A Offer to share it, then throw sand in her face and make a run for it with the supplies.
B Make a genuine offer to share the booty.
C Offer her all the supplies and agree that she saw them first.
D Surrender with all your supplies.

7 Zombies can be best described as:

A Creatures which must be destroyed.
B Humans suffering from the zombic condition.
C The 'mortally challenged' – they're people too you know.
D Made-up creatures called Edward or Jacob.

8 You encounter a group of UN soldiers. They say they are evacuating people, starting with the elderly. Do you?

A Dress in a cardigan and limp through their checkpoint as if you are 80.
B Applaud their rescue attempt and help them to guard the complex.
C Offer to help in their medical tent.
D Agree to help search for elderly survivors.

9 Which answer best summarizes your approach to the zombie apocalypse:

A I'm armed, trained and ready for it to kick off. In fact, I'm quite looking forward to it.
B I'm fearful. I've made some preparations, but my social life keeps getting in the way.
C I've bought all the books and plan to read them later.
D Zombies don't exist so it's not worth doing any planning.

10 Your ideal role during the zombie apocalypse is:

A A powerful baron of the zombie apocalypse, with hundreds of fighters at my disposal.
B A key member of the anti-zombie army, fighting to liberate the country.
C I want to use it as a chance to develop myself in so many areas.
D I want to join the undead and start sparkling in the sunshine.

11 Your perfect weapon against the zombies is:

A Anything that enables me to kill the most zombies or survivors if they get in my way.
B A trusty clubbing weapon, easy to carry and robust.
C I'd carry a long stick so I could poke the zombies away. I prefer not to kill.
D I never carry weapons, I'm a pacifist.

12 What is the Zombie Clearing System?

A A way to bash every undead zombie in an area.
B A strategy to clear zombies from an area.
C It's using trains to get rid of the dead.
D It's some kind of soap for cleaning the dead.

MINISTRY OF ZOMBIES

13 **You see a group of zombies breaking into a house you know is occupied by a small group of survivors. Do you?**

A Keep watch and see if the zombies get in. You might be able to pick up some supplies later.

B Try to warn the group without drawing attention to yourself.

C Shout a warning to them, fearless for your own safety.

D Run towards the besieging zombies then wait for the survivors to join you in battle.

14 **You are caught by a giant zombie and you are unarmed. Do you?**

A Take on the zombie in hand-to-hand combat? No dead man is going to get the better of you.

B Look for the chance to make a run for it. Unarmed combat against the dead is for lunatics.

C Distract the creature by throwing your voice.

D Reason with the creature and back away.

15 **Your perfect zombie survival team is?**

A Like the stunt doubles from the *Expendables*. All hard cases with a crazy desire to kill.

B A balanced set of survivals with valuable medical, combat and survival skills.

C All my best friends and that person at work.

D A group of non-violent vegans who just want to make the world a better place.

16 **There are four survivors outside and you have room for one. Which one do you take in?**

A The Military guy – he's got guns and the skills you need.

B The Mechanic girl – she can help you fix up that car.

C The Lawyer.

D The most vulnerable as they need more help.

17 **The Zombie War will be won by:**

A Killing each and every zombie, regardless of the human casualties.

B A co-ordinated use of survivor forces, defeating the zombies in key locations then expanding out to liberate the country.

C I'll help, but I'm not sure we'll win.

D It's fighting that got us into this mess. We should join forces together with the zombies.

18 **There is a talk on zombiology at a local college. Do you?**

A Forget about it and carry on with your weapons training.

B Check who the speaker is. If they are Ministry of Zombies approved, attend with a notepad.

C Think about going, but watch reruns of *The Walking Dead* instead.

D Go along and then make a scene, trying to convince everyone that zombies don't exist.

19 **Which statement best describes your thoughts on zombie mutations?**

A Bring it on. As long as they can be killed, I don't care what they look like.

B There is little proof around zombie mutations, but I monitor the situation and any key scientific developments.

C Mutation might be a good thing – maybe zombies will start eating grass.

D I like the X-men – they're really cool mutants. Wolverine is my favorite.

20 **Which statement best summarizes your attitude to surviving the zombies?**

A I will survive, no matter what the cost. I'd toss my Granny to the zombies if it was me or her.

B I want to survive and have the skills to do it. I want to stay human and this means helping others as well.

C I've got a better chance than most, I mean I've read most of this book and only skipped a few pages.

D Of course I want to survive. If it was all real I'd be training for at least an hour a month.

> Now count up your answers then read the profiles below. If you have scored mostly Bs you've passed, good job survivor. If you've scored mostly As then you are one dangerous character but well done, you have also passed.

YOUR SCORE • ADVANCED LEVEL

▶ MOSTLY As

You are a cruel tough guy of the apocalypse, but your survival chances are excellent. However, you could easily become a selfish scoundrel and may be foolhardy, a danger to yourself and those around you.

'THIS VIOLENT MAVERICK COULD GO EITHER WAY. ONE THING IS FOR SURE, IF ANYONE IS GOING TO SURVIVE, THEY ARE.'

▶ MOSTLY Bs

You are a balanced and well-equipped survivor, with skills and the knowledge to survive. However, there may be times you need to act firmly for the sake of the many. You will be a key player in the zombie war.

'THESE SURVIVORS ARE THE HOPE FOR US ALL. IT'S THESE FOLKS WHO WILL BE OUT THERE FIGHTING FOR THE HUMAN RACE.'

▶ MOSTLY Cs

You cannot count on surviving the opening weeks of a zombie apocalypse. You are likely to fall victim to the first gang of looters you come across. You need to study this book again and do it seriously this time.

'THERE'S POTENTIAL THERE, BUT WITHOUT ANTI-ZOMBIE EXPERTISE, IT'S LIKE A GUN WITH NO BULLETS.'

▶ MOSTLY Ds

Did you just pick the book up and turn to the quiz? You will be eaten within 24 hours of a zombie outbreak. You will be of little use to survivors. You are the walking definition of a cheap meat snack for the zombies.

'A GREAT PERSON TO GET EATEN WHILE THE REST OF US SERIOUS SURVIVORS ARE MAKING OUR ESCAPE.'

GLOSSARY

apocalypse A great disaster; a sudden and very bad event that causes much fear, loss, or destruction.

barricade (v) To block (something) so that people or things cannot enter or leave; (n) a temporary wall, fence, or similar structure that is built to prevent people from entering a place or area.

cannibal A person who eats the flesh of human beings or an animal that eats its own kind.

corpse A dead body.

decomposition The process by which dead organic matter separates into simpler substances; decay; rot.

desiccated Dried up; drained of emotional or intellectual vitality.

gastric Of, relating to, or near the stomach.

ghoul An evil creature in frightening stories that robs graves and eats dead bodies.

metamorphosis A major change in the appearance or character of someone or something ; a major change in the form or structure of some animals or insects that happens as the animal or insect becomes an adult.

mutation A significant and basic alteration; change; a relatively permanent change in hereditary material.

outbreak A sudden start or increase of fighting or disease.

perimeter The outside edge of an area or surface; a line or strip bounding or protecting an area.

plague A large number of harmful or annoying things ; a disease that causes death and that spreads quickly to a large number of people.

post-apocalyptic The period of time and disastrous conditions that follow after an apocalypse; the aftermath of a massive and highly destructive disaster.

quarantine The period of time during which a person or animal that has a disease or that might have a disease is kept away from others to prevent the disease from spreading ; the situation of being kept away from others to prevent a disease from spreading.

siege A situation in which soldiers or police officers surround a city, building, etc., in order to try to take control of it ; a serious and lasting attack of something.

survivalist A person who believes that government and society will soon fail completely and who stores food, weapons, etc., in order to be prepared to survive when that happens.

symptom A change in the body or mind which indicates that a disease is present ; a change which shows that something bad exists : a sign of something bad.

transmission The act or process by which something, such as a virus, is spread or passed from one person or thing to another.

undead A creature that has movement, volition, and will, but is not technically alive, such as a zombie or vampire, and must feed upon the living in order to continue its existence.

virus The causative agent of an infectious disease; any of a large group of submicroscopic infective agents that are regarded either as extremely simple microorganisms or as extremely complex molecules that are capable of growth and multiplication only in living cells, and that cause various important diseases in humans, lower animals, or plants.

vulnerable Easily hurt or harmed physically, mentally, or emotionally ; open to attack, harm, or damage.

FOR MORE INFORMATION

American Folklore Society
Indiana University, Eigenmann Hall
1900 East 10th Street
Bloomington, IN 47406
Phone: (812) 856-2379
Website: http://www.afsnet.org
The American Folklore Society is an association of folklorists: people who study and communicate knowledge about
folklore throughout the world. Its 2,000 members and subscribers are scholars, teachers, and libraries at colleges and
universities; professionals in arts and cultural organizations; and community members involved in folklore work. Many
of its members live and work in the U.S., but their interests in folklore stretch around the world, and today about one
in every eight AFS members is from outside the U.S. A collective of university-based humanities scholars, museum
anthropologists, and private citizens—including author Mark Twain and US President Rutherford B. Hayes—founded
the Society in Cambridge, MA, in 1888.

Center for Disease Control and Prevention
Office of Public Health Preparedness and Response
1600 Clifton Road Atlanta, GA 30329-4027
Phone: 800-CDC-INFO (800-232-4636)
Website: http://www.cdc.gov/phpr/index.htm
The Office of Public Health Preparedness and Response (PHPR) is committed to strengthening the nation's health
security by saving lives and protecting against public health threats, whether at home or abroad, natural or human-
made. Health security depends on the ability of our nation to prevent, protect against, mitigate, respond to, and
recover from public health threats. To ensure that, PHPR supports state, local, tribal, and territorial partners by
providing funding, building capacity, offering technical assistance, and championing their critical role in protecting the
public's health.

Center for Disease Control and Prevention's Zombie Preparedness Web Page
1600 Clifton Road
Atlanta, GA 30329-4027
Phone: 800-CDC-INFO (800-232-4636)
Website: http://www.cdc.gov/phpr/zombies.htm
http://blogs.cdc.gov/publichealthmatters/2011/05/preparedness-101-zombie-apocalypse/
What first began as a tongue in cheek campaign by the Center for Disease Control and Prevention to engage new
audiences with preparedness messages has proven to be a very effective platform. It continues to reach and engage
a wide variety of audiences on all hazards preparedness via Zombie Preparedness.

Center for Folklore Studies
The Ohio State University
1961 Tuttle Park Place
Columbus, OH 43210
Phone: (614) 292-1639
Website: https://cfs.osu.edu/about
The Center for Folklore Studies at the Ohio State University supports the learning, teaching, research, and outreach
of folklorists and students of folklore. With participation from across the colleges of Arts and Humanities, Social
and Behavioral Sciences, and Education and Human Ecology, the Center provides folklorists with a network for
cooperation and interdisciplinary dialogue.

FOR MORE INFORMATION

The Folklore Society,
c/o The Warburg Institute
Woburn Square
London WC1H 0AB, UK
Phone: +44 (0) 207 862 8564
Website: http://folklore-society.com

The Folklore Society (FLS) is a scholarly society devoted to the study of traditional culture in all its forms. It was founded in London in 1878 and was one of the first organizations established in the world for the study of folklore. The Folklore Society's interest and expertise covers such topics as traditional music, song, dance and drama, narrative, arts and crafts, customs, and belief. It is also interested in popular religion, traditional and regional food, folk medicine, children's folklore, traditional sayings, proverbs, rhymes, and jingles. Its aims are to foster the research and documentation of folklore worldwide, and to make the results of such study available to all, whether members of the Society or not.

Zombie Research Society (ZRS)
Contact: Mogk@ZRS.me
Website: http://zombieresearchsociety.com

Zombie Research Society (ZRS) was founded in 2007 as an organization dedicated to the historic, cultural, and scientific study of the living dead. The organization has grown to include hundreds of thousands of active members across the world. Its team of experts currently consists of a number of prominent authors, artists, and academics committed to the real-life research of zombies and the undead, as well as a core group of volunteers who handle the daily management of ZRS.

Zombie Squad, Inc.
P.O. Box 63124
St. Louis, MO 63163-3124
Email: chapters@zombiehunters.org
Phone: (888) 495-4052
Website: https://www.zombiehunters.org

Zombie Squad is the world's pre-eminent non-stationary cadaver suppression task force, committed to helping defend your neighborhood and town from the hordes of the undead. It provides trained and motivated highly-skilled zombie suppression professionals as well as zombie survival consultants.

Web sites

Due to the changing nature of Internet links, Rosen Publishing has developed an online list of Web sites related to the subject of this book. This site is updated regularly. Please use this link to access this list:

http://www.rosenlinks.com/SZW/Spot

FOR FURTHER READING

Austin, John. So Now You're a Zombie: A Handbook for the Newly Undead. Chicago, IL: Chicago Review Press, 2010.

Borgenicht, David, and Ben H. Winters. The Worst-Case Scenario Survival Handbook: Paranormal. San Francisco, CA: Chronicle Books, 2011.

Brooks, Max. World War Z: An Oral History of the Zombie War. New York, NY: Three Rivers Press, 2007.

Brooks, Max. The Zombie Survival Guide: Complete Protection from the Living Dead. New York, NY: Broadway Books, 2003.

Emerson, Clint. 100 Deadly Skills: The SEAL Operative's Guide to Eluding Pursuers, Evading Capture, and Surviving Any Dangerous Situation. New York, NY: Touchstone, 2015.

Lonely Planet. How to Survive Anything: A Visual Guide to Laughing in the Face of Adversity. Oakland, CA: Lonely Planet, 2015.

Luckhurst, Roger. Zombies: A Cultural History. London, England: Reaktion, Books, 2015.

Ma, Roger. The Zombie Combat Manual: A Guide to Fighting the Living Dead. New York, NY: Berkley, 2010.

MacWelch, Tim, and the editors of Outdoor Life. How to Survive Anything: From Animal Attacks to the End of the World (and Everything in Between). San Francisco, CA: Weldon Owen, 2015.

MacWelch, Tim, and the editors of Outdoor Life. Prepare for Anything Survival Manual: 338 Essential Skills. San Francisco, CA: Weldon Owen, 2014.

Mogk, Matt. Everything You Ever Wanted to Know About Zombies. New York, NY: Gallery Books, 2011.

Piven, Joshua, and David Borgenicht. The Complete Worst-Case Scenario Survival Handbook. San Francisco, CA: Chronicle Books, 2007.

Piven, Joshua, and David Borgenicht. The Worst-Case Scenario Survival Handbook: Extreme Edition. San Francisco, CA: Chronicle Books, 2005.

Rawles, James Wesley. How to Survive the End of the World as We Know It: Tactics, Techniques, and Technologies for Uncertain Times. New York, NY: Penguin Books, 2009.

Wilson, Lauren, and Kristian Bauthus. The Art of Eating Through the Zombie Apocalypse: A Cookbook and Culinary Survival Guide. Dallas, TX: Smart Pop, 2014.

Wiseman, John "Lofty." SAS Survival Handbook: The Ultimate Guide to Surviving Anywhere. New York, NY: William Morrow, 2014.

INDEX

A

Ahmed, Dr. Khalid, 8, 12, 13, 21
anti-zombie products, 34–35
Australia, accounts of zombies
    in, 22

B

Banjo Brand products, 34, 35
Bite-Away, 34
body suit, zombie-proof, 35
Bug-Out Bag, 18, 26, 30–31, 33
Bug-Out Locations, 30, 32, 33
Bug-Out Plan, 30, 31, 33

C

cemeteries, zombies and, 11
climatic conditions, and types of
    zombies, 9

E

Epic of Gilgamesh, The, 20

M

Macgregor's Farm, Siege at, 22
Monroe's Zombie Pellets, 34
mutation of zombie virus, 15

R

Roman Empire, accounts of
    zombies in, 22, 23
Romero, George, 15

S

survival exams
        dvanced level, 40–41
        basic level, 38–39
survivalist, zombie
    advice for those with
        disabilities, 31
    getting the look of, 28–29
    signs you are ready to be,
        27
survivor team, building, 36–37

T

28 Days Later, 15

U

Uncle Ted's Anti-Ghoul Tonic, 35

V

vampires, zombies vs., 11
Vietnam, accounts of zombies
    in, 22

W

warning scale, of zombie
    apocalypse, 25

Z

Zombie History of Europe, A, 22
Zombie Knowledge Triangle, 6
zombies
    characteristics of, 6, 7
    common misconceptions
      about, 11
    cure for, 12, 14
    in history, 20–23
    how to kill, 10–11
    how to spot, 7
    mutations of, 15
    transformation/evolution of,
      8–9, 12–13
    types of, 8–9
Zombies, Ministry of, 6, 18, 21,
    28, 30, 31, 32, 33, 34, 36, 39,
    41
zombie virus
    and animals, 18–19
    facts about, 14
    mutation of, 15
zombiology, science of, 12–13

AUTHOR'S ACKNOWLEDGMENTS

I hope you enjoy reading this book as much as we all did writing, designing and illustrating it. When we started, there were unbelievers working on the team, now we are all ready for the zombie apocalypse and slightly more paranoid than before. I want to thank my partners in crime Louise and Richard at Haynes for all their hard work and patience – both were last seen heading for their secure locations in Scotland. Also, to my wife for her tireless support as we spent weekends testing everything from crossbows to living in a sealed concrete bunker – see my website for details and more insanity – www.ministryofzombies.com. Finally, I want to mention all my family back in Ashford. I come from a close family – not in a weird or banjo-playing way – we just get along and this book is dedicated to them and my home-town.

⚠ WARNING!